4TH GRADE(R)
(Age 9)

Life's Turning Point

Bobb Biehl and Emőke Tapolyai

Written for: *Counselors | Grandparents | Leaders | Managers | Parents | Pastors | Teachers | You*

© 2020 by Bobb Biehl

All rights reserved
Printed in the United States of America

Published by Aylen Publishing
7830 E. Camelback Road, Ste. 711
Scottsdale, AZ 85251
ISBN: 978-0-9857708-8-4

Fourth Grade

TABLE OF CONTENTS

A. INTRODUCTION

We are a presidential mentor and a psychologist, not teachers, professors, researchers or coaches …

… but we have seen consistent patterns.

B. WHY IS THE FOURTH GRADE THE TURNING POINT?

1. Age 9/fourth grade is the year of the "adult child."

2. Is it actually age 9 or the fourth grade?

3. Age 9/fourth-graders are:

    - Old enough to "get it."
    - Young enough to "believe it."
    - Regardless of who "says it"!

4. Age 9/fourth-grade experiences shape our "adult comfort zones"!

5. Age 9/fourth-graders need adult observation, strengthening, and protection!

6. Age 9/fourth-graders find it easy to memorize; take advantage of this window of opportunity.

7. Age 9/fourth grade: What if I can't remember my fourth grade?

C. YOUR FOURTH-GRADER'S SHAPING POINTS

- *Age 9 is shaping your child's adult* LIFE VALUES.

- *Age 9 is shaping your child's adult* ACADEMIC COMFORT.

- *Age 9 is shaping your child's adult* WORKPLACE LEADERSHIP ROLE.

- *Age 9 is shaping your child's adult* NEIGHBORHOOD ROLE.

- *Age 9 is shaping your child's adult* COMMUNITY COMMITMENTS.

- *Age 9 is shaping your child's adult* FAMILY CHEMISTRY.

- *Age 9 is shaping your child's adult* GENDER RELATIONSHIPS.

- *Age 9 is shaping your child's adult* COMPETITIVENESS.

- *Age 9 is shaping your child's adult*
  CLOSE FRIENDSHIP PATTERN.

- *Age 9 is shaping your child's adult*
  LIFE ORIENTATION.

D. TAKING ADVANTAGE
of understanding the fourth-grade turning points

1. Parents: Raising a fourth-grader.

2. Aunts, Uncles, Grandparents:
   Helping parents raise a fourth-grader.

3. Clergy, Coaches, Educators:
   Helping parents raise fourth-graders.

4. Today: Fourth-grade implications for dating and marriage.

5. Today: Fourth-grade implications for building a strong team.

6. Today: Overcoming a traumatic fourth grade.

E. QUESTIONS AND ANSWERS

F. WRAP-UP

Fourth Grade

A. INTRODUCTION

As authors we are not teachers, professors, researchers or athletic coaches. At the same time, we have seen very consistent patterns between fourth grade (age 9) experiences and adult comfort zones.

BOBB: As a presidential mentor, I have consulted with approximately 500 companies. I have spent approximately 5,000 hours with executives at many levels. Over those thousands of one-to-one hours I have observed consistent and predictable patterns linking the fourth grade and adult comfort zones.

My wife and I also have two children, three grandchildren and four great-grandchildren.
We have had the opportunity to watch many fourth-graders in action!

EMŐKE: As a psychologist, I have often seen a very clear relationship between an adult's emotional struggles and the patient's fourth-grade experiences. As a clinical counselor who grew up, lived and now practices in Budapest, Hungary, I can testify with confidence that the age 9 turning point is cross-cultural. The fourth-grade establishment of comfort zones, and its influence on adult behavior, is simply a human phenomenon. I also have five children.

We have had the opportunity to watch many fourth-graders in action!

Fourth Grade

Fourth Grade

B. WHY IS THE FOURTH GRADE THE TURNING POINT?

> *Age 9 (typically the fourth grade) is the turning point that establishes our adult comfort zones.*

1. Age 9/fourth grade is the year of the "adult child."

BOBB: A few years ago, on a whim I started asking my adult consulting clients to tell me about some of the shaping events in their life. They would predictably ask me, "Do you mean like childhood experiences?" I would answer, "Just go back as far as you care to, covering some of the shaping events in your life."

After giving approximately a hundred executives this assignment, I began to see a very predictable pattern. Approximately 80 percent would look up at the ceiling, take a few seconds, look directly into my eyes and then with excitement in their voice say, "I must have been in the fourth grade when ..." Then they would go on to explain an early life-shaping event they remembered. This pattern began to really fascinate me. Why so predictably the fourth grade?

One day I was consulting with Dr. Robert Lewis, then the teaching pastor of Fellowship Bible Church in Little Rock, Arkansas, now the founder of Men's

Fourth Grade

Fraternity. We were walking through the church lobby on our way to his study when Robert said, "Bobb, I'd like to introduce you to the newest member of our team. Last year she was voted the teacher of the year in Arkansas. She taught fourth grade ..."

That was all I needed to hear. I immediately asked if I could have five minutes with her. After the introduction, Robert went back to his study and after a few seconds of casual conversation I got to my burning question:

"I know the fourth grade is a turning point year in a person's life but why is the fourth grade so very shaping?"

"Oh, that's easy," was her immediate response. *"The fourth grade is the year of the 'adult child.'"*

THIRD-GRADERS:

- Are still little children in their hearts and in their brains.
- They are little children in their hearts in that they naively believe whatever someone tells them.
- Their brains are not developed enough to really concentrate.

  They are always fiddling with something or distracted by anything going past.

  To really understand, comprehend, and remember much, you need to be able to concentrate.

- Third-graders are managed with "close supervision" on the playground, with a teacher close at hand to insist, "Don't hit her/him; how would you feel if she/he hit you?"

FOURTH-GRADERS:
- Are still little children in their hearts; they still believe whatever you tell them!
- But their brains are developed to the point where they can concentrate, comprehend and carry on almost adult conversations. They can remember what they hear and experience!
- They have a delightful combination of an adult's head and a child's heart — thus the phrase "adult child."
- The fourth grade is also the first time children are given general supervision on the playground with the teachers saying, "Go play and don't come back until you hear the bell."

  They are left to fend for themselves and make their own way on the playground!

FIFTH-GRADERS:
- Are no longer children in their hearts; they are moving toward the teen years.
- Fifth-graders can concentrate and argue with you on various subjects and believe nothing just because you say it is so.

- They are not yet mature adults — but they are no longer little children in their hearts or their heads; they are on their way to becoming teenagers!

The fourth grade is a little protected period in which children are smart enough to get it and naive enough to accept it and their lives are typically simple enough not to be cluttered with a lot of other distractions. The Arkansas teacher added, "We hate to see the tenderhearted fourth-graders leave each year because fifth-graders come back. Fourth-graders are easy to teach compared to the more questioning, more defensive, more sophisticated, no-longer-children fifth-graders!"

2. Is it actually age 9 or the fourth grade?

You may ask, "Is the magic phase of life actually age 9 or is it the fourth grade?"

If you ask the next 100 adults you meet about the role they played on the playground at age 9, the very first question you can expect from these 100 folks is, "What grade was that?"

It is actually age 9 that is such a shaping year.

So if a child is held back or skipped a grade, it may be her or his third or fifth grade.

Fourth Grade

If your fourth-grader is just not quite mature enough to be with the class from your perspective, it may be better to hold them back a year and let them re-establish. This is particularly true if you're going to be moving or if they are changing schools — hold them back one year. At 9 years old, they are still young enough to adjust to those new relationships. They can get to where they are as mature as their peers, not behind their peers.

We would also suggest you not start children in school early. By the time they're 9, they're in the fifth grade, and they never feel quite confident socially. They may be mentally and academically confident, but emotionally they don't fit quite yet. We would start children late rather than early.

3. At age 9, fourth-graders are:

- **Old enough to "get it."**
- **Young enough to "believe it."**
- **Regardless of who "says it"!**

Whenever anyone says something about them, good or bad, a fourth-grader understands and believes it to be true — frequently remembering it for a lifetime! When a parent, teacher, coach, or a relative says, "You are beautiful, smart, talented, and going to be great!" the child understands it, naively believes it, and remembers it!

Fourth Grade

But the opposite is, unfortunately, also true. When a parent, teacher, coach, or a relative says, "You are ugly, dumb, clumsy, and going to jail someday!" the child understands it, naively believes it, and remembers it!

In a wide variety of cases, unfortunately, it is also true that when an unthinking brother, sister, or bully kid on the playground says, "You are ugly, dumb, clumsy, and going to jail some day!" the child understands it, naively believes it, and remembers it from those voices as well.

Fourth-graders are still very vulnerable to being defined and, in adulthood, confined by the expectations and comments from all around them.

Look for the right time to talk to your fourth-grader. Most fourth-graders have a certain time of day (or night) when they are very talkative. It may be late in the evening when you are very tired and do not feel at all like chatting about their day. Be very careful right here. When you feel like it is the right time for you, they may not be in the mood to talk at all. Look for the time when they want to talk about any subject you really want to discuss with them!

Let us tell you another secret about relating to fourth-graders. Many also love to cook! If you really want to find a great talking time, consider inviting them to cook something with you and talk to them while cooking.

BOBB: One of my early mentors offered this great insight. He said, "Bobb, people learn best when they think what you are saying is not important — their defenses are not up — and they can really listen." While you are cooking you can slip in all kinds of life lessons that they think are not really that important, but they will remember them for a lifetime!

Another point to remember is that kids remember songs longer than almost anything. Sing a song with and for your fourth-grader that you would like them to remember with very positive emotions for the rest of their life. Think about it. You do not have to be a great singer, it is creating a great memory!

At this age a wide variety of voices are telling them who they are and what they should or should not do. Fourth-graders begin to look for comfort zones where they are doing what is expected of them, where they fit, where they belong, where they are doing it right and where they will not be yelled at or made fun of — by anyone!

For the first time in a child's life, he or she goes out and starts trying to fit into the society of the playground without constant or direct adult supervision. The child may start trying to lead, only to have another stronger, more dominant child say, "You're not the leader!" If a bigger kid on the playground says, "Go sit down, you are not good at this sport," or they are the last chosen, they assume it must be true and often simply feel more comfortable playing by themselves or playing a different game with different children.

Fourth Grade

On the other hand, some are selected as leaders on the playground. Other kids say, "You're the leader, tell us what to do." In this situation, the child often begins to assume, "I must be a leader or they wouldn't be saying that, so I guess I'll start leading." And they get comfortable being a leader on the playground.

As fourth-graders, children begin to discover where they fall in this playground pecking order. The pecking order of the playground is set up for the first time in the fourth grade. It is established by natural chemistry and natural leadership in the fourth grade. The fourth grade is when we begin to sense if and where we should be leaders or followers. We become aware that other children will do what we tell them to do — or not!

Around home, fourth-graders are typically allowed more freedom as well. Children may be allowed to ride their bikes around the neighborhood for the first time. They "sleep over" at friends' homes.

The fourth grade is a turning point year of being in the society of other children without adults constantly telling them what to do or how to act or what role they are to play.

Many children never see themselves as leaders in any area. But there are a wide variety of other areas in which your child can lead:

- Church.
- Classroom.

- Neighborhood after school.
- Playground.
- Scouting.
- Siblings … and many more.

If you find your child resisting leadership roles, this is also a time to encourage them that it is OK to be a follower. Children and especially teenagers often hear that in order to fit into society, they need to be leaders. It is important to let them know that followers and team members are a needed part of a group. The fourth grade is a time when you can plant the message in their heart that being a team member can also be valuable. Later it will help them when they will be under the stress of society's expectations.

4. Age 9/fourth-grade experiences shape our adult comfort zones!

You may think we are the least likely individuals to write a book about the fourth-grade connection to our adult comfort zones. You may ask, "What makes you the experts?"

We are not child development experts. We are not currently the parents of fourth-graders. Our children are now grown. We are not fourth-grade Sunday school teachers nor are we fourth-grade elementary teachers or school principals.

As mentioned earlier, years ago as we started asking questions about leadership styles, staff relationships,

Fourth Grade

executive fears, marital relationships, and other concerns, the conversation eventually drifted back to what happened in childhood.

Over the past decade it has become obvious that what the executives are comfortable doing today is what they were comfortable doing in the fourth grade. If they were not comfortable leading or following in the fourth grade, they are not comfortable leading or following today.

As adults we live a very high percentage of the time in our comfort zones. No one likes getting too far out beyond her or his comfort zones. Over the past decade we have found a very high correlation between the fourth grade and our adult comfort zones!

In your mature adult years, you will find that the correlation between your fourth-grade comfort zones and your adult comfort zones is far greater than that between your adult comfort zones and what we refer to as the "years of the masks": your pre-teen, teen and young adult years.

Where a child is successful, they come to feel comfortable.

They tend to stay in the comfort zone for hours and hours — becoming more and more comfortable and competent in that zone.

We tend to return to these very same comfort zones as adults — especially under the pressures of adult life.

Often the child who is only or primarily comfortable *alone* ends up needing time as an adult — *alone*!

Often the child who is only or primarily comfortable *at church* ends up somewhere *in ministry*.

Often the child who is only or primarily comfortable *in the classroom* ends up somewhere *in education*.

Often the child who is only or primarily comfortable leading *in the neighborhood* ends up *starting her or his own organization or corporation* — where they can decide who they work with on a daily basis.

Often the child who is only or primarily comfortable *reading* ends up needing a lot of time as an adult *reading* in a comfortable, quiet,

Fourth Grade

> safe place.
>
> Often the child who is only or primarily comfortable in ***scouting*** ends up ***an adult scout leader*** — or some other field where they can wear a comfortable and respected uniform.
>
> This does not mean as an adult we cannot do other things. But it does mean that when we are tired, under pressure, or given the option, we will revert to our fourth-grade comfort zones.

5. Age 9 fourth-graders need adult observation, strengthening, and protection!

The fourth grade is the unique window where you, as an adult, need to be involved in the development of your fourth-grader. Being involved in their development is not manipulative; it is simply helping your child grow to their full, healthy, balanced potential.

Watch carefully as your fourth-grader develops. You observe things as an adult they do not see, understand, or know how to cope with on a daily basis. As you watch them developing, if you see negative patterns, if you see insecurities, if you see problems that could become major problems in her or his life as an adult, step in!

Here are just a few of the hundreds of ways to strengthen a child:

- Giving them positive verbal affirmation.
- Pointing out their specific strengths.
- Spending time with them, helping develop their strengths.
- Talking with them — asking them questions (covered later in this book) to get a feel for their strengths.

Also, as adults it is our responsibility to help protect our fourth-graders. If we see them being bullied, assigned to a cruel or belittling teacher, intimidated by a demanding coach at an unrealistic level, or being treated cruelly on the playground (to name just a few threats), we need to step in!

Many parents do not let their child be alone with another adult person (even seemingly the most easily trusted) who may be a child molester. That is likely a wise policy.

Use your wise judgment. It is not inappropriate or manipulative to step in if you see your fourth-grader experiencing things that can inhibit mature development as adults.

6. Age 9 fourth-graders find it easy to memorize; take advantage of this window of opportunity.

This is the year when memorization is typically very easy.

BOBB: One day I asked the then president of AWANA, the worldwide children's program, in what grade kids are able to memorize the most Scripture. He instantly responded, "The fourth grade."

In the third grade, the mind is not developed enough to really concentrate and really understand adult concepts. A brilliant client of mine, a writer, author and speaker, has memorized massive amounts of complicated material. One day in casual conversation I asked him, "What's the key to your incredible ability to memorize?" His immediate one-word answer: "Concentration!" He went on to explain:

"If you can't concentrate, you can't memorize."

By the fourth grade, children's brains are developed to a point where they can concentrate and "get" a lot of what is going on; their minds are not yet distracted by a lot of pre-teen social awkwardness. They can concentrate — and remember!

Consider having a very specific memory program for them in the fourth grade: facts, geography, principles, Scripture memory verses, languages, songs, etc. Stop for a minute and ask yourself, "What are the top principles, songs, thoughts, Scripture verses, etc., I'd like my fourth-grader to remember for a lifetime?"

7. Age 9/fourth grade: "What if I don't even remember the fourth grade?"

Hundreds of executives have told us the shaping experiences of their childhoods. However, their initial response is often, "That's too far back. I cannot remember my childhood." They think we're looking for extremely detailed descriptions of every aspect of their childhood.

We assure them, "We're in no rush; take some time. Can you remember the country you lived in? (They typically chuckle and say "Of course." "Can you remember the school you attended?" ("Yes," they answer.) "The house you lived in?" ("Yes.") "Who some of your little friends were at that time?" ("Yes.") If you can remember that much, you remember enough to take advantage of the insights of this book.

We continue, "Talk about some of the shaping events of your childhood." They look off into space for between 30 to 60 seconds, and then they say, "I've got it! I remember — I must have been in about the fourth grade, when (they name another person) said or did something that left a mark on my mind."

Then they have a detailed emotional memory of the fourth grade, and they begin to see what we mean. We are not sure if they fully grasp it right away, but they can immediately begin to see the parallels between what they were doing in the fourth grade and what they are comfortable doing as an adult.

Fourth Grade

C. YOUR FOURTH-GRADER'S SHAPING POINTS

We all have comfort zones as adults that were shaped in our lives as fourth-graders. These comfort zones are areas in which we prefer living our lives. These are the areas in which we are very comfortable and experience very little stress.

Areas in which we feel comfortable and relaxed as children and experience positive success are where we find it natural to function as adults. This does not say we cannot function in areas that are not our natural comfort zones. However, when we get fatigued, stressed, or under pressure, we tend to revert to our comfort zones — established in the fourth grade.

We have found at least 10 areas of life in which a child's adult comfort zones are being shaped in her or his ninth year, typically in the fourth grade.

1. *Age 9 is shaping your child's adult* **LIFE VALUES.**

2. *Age 9 is shaping your child's adult* **ACADEMIC COMFORT.**

3. *Age 9 is shaping your child's adult* **WORKPLACE LEADERSHIP ROLE.**

4. *Age 9 is shaping your child's adult* **NEIGHBORHOOD ROLE.**

Fourth Grade

5. *Age 9 is shaping your child's adult* **COMMUNITY COMMITMENTS.**

6. *Age 9 is shaping your child's adult* **FAMILY CHEMISTRY.**

7. *Age 9 is shaping your child's adult* **GENDER RELATIONSHIPS.**

8. *Age 9 is shaping your child's adult* **COMPETITIVENESS.**

9. *Age 9 is shaping your child's adult* **CLOSE FRIENDSHIP PATTERN.**

10. *Age 9 is shaping your child's adult* **LIFE ORIENTATION.**

As a mature adult you will feel far more comfortable in your fourth-grade comfort zones! The further you get from your true fourth-grade comfort zones, the more stress you will feel.

To help you see how shaping your daughter's or son's fourth-grade experience is, we would like to help you see how much your age 9 (fourth grade) experiences shaped your adult comfort zones. If you can see the connections between your own fourth-grade experiences and your adult comfort zones, you will have new eyes to see the implications of what your children and all of the children your life influences are experiencing and how shaping it is for their entire adult life!

Fourth Grade

In this section of the book, we will look at 10 of the common adult comfort zones shaped in the fourth grade that we have seen over and over.

1. *Age 9 is shaping your child's adult*

LIFE VALUES

As a mature adult today looking back on your fourth grade ...

>What was your father's first name? _____
>Occupation? _____
>
>What was your mother's first name? _____
>Occupation? _____
>
>Watching your dad in the fourth grade, what were the three most important things to him?
>_____
>_____
>_____
>
>Watching your mom in the fourth grade, what were the three most important things to her?
>_____
>_____
>_____

What are your most deeply held values today?

How important are the above six life values to you today?

Your life values were unconsciously being shaped in your fourth-grade experience by what you saw modeled by the primary adults in your world.

Common patterns we have seen with our clients:
(Bobb's consulting and Emöke's counseling)

- Watching is far more powerful than listening. There is a high percentage of alignment between what we watched our parents know, do, and become and what we see as important as adults.
- By age 9, a child can identify what is actually valued by the "mother's side of the family" as compared to the "father's side of the family."

  The child picks up adult values from both sides of the family.
- An adult can put into a few words what was most valuable to each side of the family.
- An adult can typically identify what they learned from each side of the family.
- If a child did not live with parents, ask, "Who was the most dominant male or female figure who cared for you in the fourth grade?"

  Ask, "What did you learn by watching these adults in your fourth grade?"

- Often a fourth-grader sees the difference between parents that were on a salary and parents who had no salary. A parent on salary typically represented financial security — low risk. Parents who had no salary represented lack of financial insecurity — but an eye toward entrepreneurial opportunity.

CASE STUDY — Emőke

Haley grew up in a small town with farmer parents. Although she had more responsibilities than most children her age, her mother kept telling her to take a break and go play after finishing her chores. She remembers her parents telling her how they wanted her to grow up and travel and enjoy life, and they wanted to provide for that. They often talked about the beauty of life and fun. However, she never saw them taking a day off other than Sundays and she never saw them leaving on vacation or going out and traveling together. Haley came to see me with severe burnout. She works in an internationally known company as a project manager. She never takes time off, often takes over the responsibility of her team members and literally burned herself out with all the work and duties. When asked about her last vacation she replied, "I do not remember when it was — maybe four or five years ago?" It's an extreme and very obvious example of how **Haley never learned the lesson her parents taught verbally but learned the lesson her parents taught by their example.**

Fourth Grade

Questions to ask your child, to understand what he or she is seeing you modeling today. And with these questions you can also start conversations to help shape your child's values:

> What do you think is really important to me as you watch me/us?

> What else? What else? What else?

How to maximize your fourth-grader today

- Make sure your values are what you want your fourth-grader to copy.

- Consistently model *(not just talk about)* the values you want your fourth-graders to have as adults.

- Discuss the advantages of your extended family's values and your mate's extended family's values.

2. *Age 9 is shaping your child's adult*

ACADEMIC COMFORT

As a mature adult today looking back on your fourth grade ...

- What was your role in the classroom?
  For example:

Fourth Grade

> Were you a straight-A student, class clown, teacher's pet, or the lowest student?

- How did you feel in the classroom?
  For example:
  > Very safe, uncomfortable, insecure, a loser?

What is your comfort level in an academic setting today?

Can you see a parallel between how you saw yourself and how you felt in the fourth-grade classroom, and how you see yourself and how you feel in an academic setting today?

Here are some very common patterns we have seen with our clients.

1. *Role* in the classroom

Fourth Grade	Mature Adult
Straight-A student.	Very comfortable in academia.
Teacher's pet.	Very comfortable in academia, friends are often 10 years older than you.
Class clown.	Comfortable speaking/teaching in very entertaining style.

Fourth Grade

Hidden in the middle of the class	OK in classroom, don't seek academic experience.
Lower or lowest student. *(Nearsighted, had dyslexia, Attention Deficit Disorder, hearing or other common fourth-grade issues.)*	Avoid classrooms as an adult.

2. *Feeling* in the classroom

Felt very safe; may have felt safer in the classroom than any other place.	Likely in some form of educational environment today.
Uncomfortable.	Rarely seek advanced education.
Insecure, a loser, "dumb." *(Nearsighted, had dyslexia, Attention Deficit Disorder, hearing or other common fourth-grade issues.)*	Avoid academic settings if possible.

3. Two schools — classroom

One common situation in the fourth grade: the fourth-grader was moved from one school to the other midyear.

Fourth Grade

Often in their first school, the fourth-grader was a leader in the classroom. In the second school the fourth-grader was intimidated by the new situation in which he or she was not a leader in the classroom.

As an adult in a classroom situation reminding them of the first school, they feel very confident and comfortable. When they are in a situation reminding them of the second school, they get intimidated, quiet and insecure. This is very common.

4. Smart vs. academic — see a lot

Another common situation is one in which a child feels dumb, not smart, because he or she did not excel in the classroom. They may have a very high IQ but still not feel smart because they did not excel in a classroom setting. Bobb has helped many presidents of companies understand that they're very smart even though they did not excel in the fourth-grade classroom.

CASE STUDY — Emőke

Steve was one of those super-smart kids in fourth grade. He was quick to understand new lessons in class, provoke his teachers and show off with his memory and complex thinking. "I loved life and made sure everybody knew it!" he remembers. He always played as a defense player on his soccer team.

Fourth Grade

He describes his sports position as a place where he could oversee everything and manage his team with his advice. He was always the center of attention, taking on public appearances and making sure that his insights and talents were visible. Today, Steve is a well-known life coach and a very successful motivational speaker. He owns a company that is publicly highly respected for his **insights, influence and leadership.**

A question to ask your child to understand where he or she is today:

How do you feel at school?

How to maximize your fourth-grader today:

- Make sure your fourth-grader is in a good school, if possible. Help the child get a great teacher and avoid a teacher who creates a negative or threatening classroom culture.

- Validate their feelings, and show them you hear their heart. This will help in their development of growing trust with people.

- If your child is "feeling behind" in any way in the fourth grade, find out why — right away. (Double-check vision, hearing, dyslexia, ADD, etc.)

- Talk to them when you are alone. Hear their hopes and dreams. Also listen to their fears, concerns and find out if (and why) they are feeling behind or bullied.

- Note to principals: Put your very best teachers in the fourth grade. It shapes your students' view of education for their entire adult life.

3. *Age 9 is shaping your child's adult*

WORKPLACE LEADERSHIP ROLE

As a mature adult today looking back on your fourth-grade ...

When the recess bell rang and you were out on the playground, what was your role?
For example, were you:

> Leader,
> First chosen,
> Muddy middle,
> Last chosen,
> Loner,
> Or playing with just one other friend —
> > apart from the group?

You are most comfortable in a leadership role at work *(assuming you work for a company that you do not own).*

Can you see a parallel today between your role on the

Fourth Grade

playground in the fourth grade and your most comfortable work role today?

Very common patterns we have seen with our clients.

1. **We are not saying you can't play a different role; just imagining the role you may feel the most comfortable playing.**

Role on fourth-grade playground	Role at work today as an adult
"Presidential Captain" Lead everything.	Lead very comfortably at work; looking for advancement to lead at a higher and higher level
"Middle Captain" Almost always first chosen.	Realistically you are still most comfortable in a support role — at a senior vice-presidential level. Others see you as presidential material. You would still feel pressure in a presidential position. You may never want to be president.
"Strong Player" Muddy middle.	Most comfortable in the "middle of the pack"
Last chosen.	Uncomfortable when asked to lead at work

Fourth Grade

Loner	Most comfortable working alone today as an adult.
Playing with just one friend.	Working with just one friend — leading or following— as you did with your friends in the fourth grade.

2. **Two schools — playground**

   One common situation in the fourth grade is one in which the fourth-grader was moved from one school to the other midyear.

   Often in their first school, the fourth-grader was a playground leader. In the second school, the fourth-grader was intimidated by the new situation in which he or she was not a leader on the playground.

   As an adult in a workplace situation reminding them of the first school, they feel very confident and comfortable. When they are in a situation reminding them of the second school, they tend to get intimidated, quiet and insecure. This is very common.

3. **BOBB: One day I was speaking at a large church** in a very wealthy region of Southern California. After I had explained this concept, a handsome, well-dressed man came up to me with

Fourth Grade

tears in his eyes. He said, "This is one of the freest days of my life!"

Because of his tears I asked him if he would care to explain. He shared that he had always been the leader of everything. He had always told the group he did not want to be the leader but they always voted him the leader anyway. No matter what he had done the group had always voted him the leader. I was not surprised. He looks so presidential I almost wanted to resign whatever I was doing and follow him in whatever he was doing (smile).

After discussing his situation further, it turned out he had a cousin who would visit him once a year in the summer for two weeks. Whenever his cousin would come to visit, since the cousin was two years older, the cousin would let this man follow, and not have the pressure of leading. Those were the freest two weeks of his year.

In his heart of hearts, the presidential-looking man in front of me always wanted to be a follower — in a one-to-one relationship — and never experience the daily pressure of team leadership and the presidency.

I asked the man, "How would you respond if the president of a major company approached you and offered you a position as his assistant? Not in charge of the division, not in charge of the department, not in charge of staff; you would

Fourth Grade

simply be his assistant. How would you respond to such an offer?"

His response: "I would take half my current salary, move anywhere in a heartbeat for that position!"

The role we feel most comfortable playing in the fourth grade is the role we typically seek in our adult workplace!

CASE STUDY — Emőke

Pete was one of those 9-year-old boys who'd get selected for the soccer team just in the middle of the selection process, not the first pick nor the last one chosen for the team. He liked playing with older boys who led him and liked scoring for whoever selected him for his team. He describes his ninth-grade school games: "I never came up with the ideas of the games. I just liked playing as a problem solver. I made sure that whatever team I was on would win. My team always won." Today Pete is a successful risk manager. His main focus of attention is helping his company get ready for unexpected situations; he describes himself as **the midfield player who helps the company score goals.**

A question to ask your child to understand where they are today:

What do you do on the playground at school?

Fourth Grade

> *(Keep expanding the discussion until you get a clear understanding of her or his role.)*

How to maximize your fourth-grader today:

- Ideally, help them know how to (learn to) lead and follow at some level on the playground.

- Give your child a bit of adult perspective on what he or she is experiencing on the playground.

- If moved to a new school in the fourth grade, help them understand the changes at school and get started again.

- Ask them: Do you like the role you get to play? What role would you like to play? Help them play the role they want!

4. *Age 9 is shaping your child's adult*

NEIGHBORHOOD ROLE

As a mature adult today looking back on your fourth grade ...

> When you got home from school and on weekends, what was your role in your neighborhood?

Fourth Grade

What is your most comfortable role in your neighborhood today?

Are you very active in the neighborhood?

Or, do you even play a role in your neighborhood, if you didn't play a role in the neighborhood after school?

Very common patterns we have seen with our clients.

1. Often a child finds herself or himself in a position where they are not a leader at all on the school playground. School is a place in which you have to play with the children who are in the same grade.

   However, when they get home they can choose who they play with in the neighborhood. Often the loner on the school playground becomes an incredible leader after school when they can choose their playmates.

   BOBB: I had a client who said he led absolutely nothing at school on the playground. When he got home and was able to choose his playmates, he became "king of the hill" when playing all sports!

   On the playground at school, you need to play with whoever is there. After school, you can decide who you will play with and who you will not play with at all.

A person who does not lead on the school playground but is the leader after school often ends up in an entrepreneurial enterprise, or a launch phase of a program where they choose exactly who they will and will not (work) with.

2. In the neighborhood, it is important to observe whether your child is leading, following, or both. Here is where you can play an active role in making sure the child has an opportunity to play with children who are both older and younger, larger and smaller, so that they learn to lead and to follow.

   In some situations, a child playing in the neighborhood is only playing with older children and never gets an opportunity to lead, or they are always leading and never need to learn how to follow.

   The neighborhood is an area in which you can arrange for them to both lead and to follow. As your child grows into adulthood this opportunity to both lead and follow as fourth-graders becomes helpful; they mature into adults who are comfortable both leading and following.

3. When a child in the fourth grade is an only child (or has a lot of time alone as a latchkey kid, farm child, or child who came way late in a family of children), often he or she needs a considerable amount of time alone as an adult.

This does not mean they are rejecting their mate. It simply means they had a considerable amount of time alone when in the fourth grade and they are extremely comfortable (and need time) being alone. Typically, they need a fair amount of time alone as adults.

The neighborhood is an area in which a lot of social skills are also developed. These are social skills apart from the skills of relating socially at school. It is also good to go out of your way to help a child have time with other children if they are raised in an "only child" environment.

CASE STUDY — Emőke

Cheryl was a happy 9-year-old. She remembers her fourth-grade year as the one when she came up with all the new and creative ideas and organized all her friends and classmates around it. She played with all the neighbors and loved people and got them to play her games. She loved people and loved life. She was a dreamer who set out to achieve her dreams. Today she works in the beauty business and is a self-made entrepreneur. One of the most outstanding sides of her business is the way she gets people dedicated to her goals and to her business. She is indeed a **people-centered dreamer and developer.**

Fourth Grade

A question to ask your child to understand where they are today:

What do you most enjoy doing after school, with your friends, when you get home?

How to maximize your fourth-grader today:

- Be sure your fourth-grader has a chance to both lead and follow; make sure they play both with younger or smaller children and older or larger children.

- Encourage your fourth-grader to initiate activity with friends and siblings after school so they will feel comfortable with organizing activities when they become adult leaders.

- Be sure your fourth-grader plays with boys and girls so they are comfortable relating to both men and women as adults.

- Watch them play, listen to their stories and see how you can support the role they play or want to play.

Fourth Grade

5. *Age 9 is shaping your child's adult*

COMMUNITY COMMITMENTS

As a mature adult today looking back on your fourth grade ...

- How involved were you in
    Church?
    Clubs?
    Sports?
    4-H?
    Other groups?

- In which were you the most comfortable and deeply committed?

What is your most comfortable organization today?

Which are you most comfortable in, and committed to today?

Are they similar to the organizations you were most comfortable in as a child?

Very common patterns we have seen with our clients.

1. An adult is typically most comfortable in organizations in which they were deeply involved, felt comfortable and took some level of responsibility in the fourth grade. For example, the person who was very comfortable and deeply

Fourth Grade

involved in church as a fourth-grader is typically deeply involved in church as an adult.

2. There are often symbolic parallels with the organization in which fourth-graders were involved and the organizations in which they're involved as adults. A person who is deeply involved with and comfortable in Boy Scouts or Girl Scouts as a child often enjoys being involved in organizations or professions that have specific ranking and uniforms as an adult.

3. Often the fourth-grader who was deeply involved in sports outside of school is deeply involved in sports as an adult. This is the person who knows the name of each player, follows each game and perhaps coaches as well.

CASE STUDY — Emőke

I've met Jack in couple counseling. Jack grew up in a missionary family where both Jack's mom and dad came from a missionary family. This actually means that all of Jack's grandparents and parents were missionaries. It was typical for Jack to care for people or to go over to help the neighbors, stay at work to talk with someone who needed a shoulder to cry on, and do favors for anyone who needed help. Although his free use of time away from home caused him and his wife many conflicts, Jack, who is an engineer, was and is a missionary-hearted man. **He feels most comfortable in mission-like situations, in helping,** in being the missionary of situations, and he is dedicated to a small missionary organization.

A question to ask your child to understand where they are today:

> What do you really enjoy doing in groups outside of school?
>
> What do you feel most comfortable doing in groups outside of school?

How to maximize your fourth-grader today:

- Encourage your fourth-grader to participate in organizations you would like to see them in as adults. Try hard to help them have great adult models and a very positive experience.

- Protect your fourth-grader from negative experiences at church. Pastor, put your best teachers in the fourth grade. The fourth-grader's adult view of the church is being shaped in the fourth-grade classroom today.

- Help them lead and follow — playing with both younger and older friends in key organizations today, if possible.

Fourth Grade

6. *Age 9 is shaping your child's adult*

CHEMISTRY

As a mature adult today looking back on your fourth grade ...

> When you were 9 years old, how many brothers and sisters did you have?
>
> What were their ages?
>
> In a few words, how would you describe your relationship with each when you were 9?

What is your most comfortable role in the family today?

> Is your role in the family the one you played in the fourth grade? Or is it the one you *wanted* to play in the fourth grade?

Common patterns we have seen with our clients.

1. We have seen very frequent patterns over and over in dealing with children in certain childhood positions:

- Oldest children — Typically feel responsible for all of the other children in the family; they cannot relax, they feel far too responsible

- Middle children — Typically feel ignored; they

feel the older child gets everything and the younger child is the favored and they are simply left out, overlooked.

- Youngest children — The youngest child is often seen as spoiled by other members of the family. They seem to get everything the older children never got. They seem to "have privileges we never had."

- Only children — Often feel lonely, wishing they had brothers and sisters to play with, fight with, do anything with so they would not have to be alone. The child who was the late-coming "surprise" often feels like an only child because their next older brother or sister is far too old to be a playmate.

2. When an adult relationship at work reminds a person of a fourth-grade relationship with a brother or sister, often there is a transference of emotion.

    If the relationship is positive, work goes well. However, if the relationship was negative in the fourth grade, often an adult work relationship with a manager begets a negative attitude that neither person can really quite understand.

    The manager wonders, "Why does this staff person respond to me the way they do?" The "adult fourth-grader" wonders, "Why am I responding to this person like I am? They've done nothing wrong to me."

The reality is simply an emotional transference from a fourth-grade relationship. For example, if a fourth-grader had an older brother who had a bullying type personality, the adult at work will not do well with a strong team leader to whom they report. They will assume and resist bullying when realistically there is simply strong leadership. They will act and react very similarly as an adult to the way they acted and reacted to their older brother as a fourth-grader.

Adult work relationships often experience a positive or negative emotional transference from a fourth-grade sibling relationship.

3. Often adult relationships with the siblings retain the same pecking order they had in the fourth grade.

BOBB: I will never forget the television interview I saw with two brothers. One of the brothers was approximately six feet, four inches tall and weighed about 280 pounds. The other brother was approximately five feet, six inches tall and weighed about 160 pounds.

As the interview went on the shorter brother kept referring to the taller, larger brother as "Tiny."

The interviewer stopped and asked the shorter

Fourth Grade

brother, "Why do you keep calling your brother 'Tiny'?" The shorter brother responded, "Oh, I guess he really isn't tiny anymore."

It was as though the shorter brother had never stopped to realize what had happened to their relative size since they were children and the baby brother was actually "tiny."

It is common for the older brother or sister to still feel responsible for the entire family. This is true even if the younger brother or sister is now the president of a major corporation.

Often the emotional "pecking order" remains the same, regardless of age.

CASE STUDY — Emőke

It is common in my work to ask people about their **place in the family**. One of my favorite stories is about a young couple, Bill and Desi. Bill, the husband, was the youngest of four children; Desi, the wife, was the oldest of four. What family dynamics! Most of their fights were about (you guessed it) who takes responsibility for what. Bill was happy with leaving any work to the side and he could not understand why Desi would want to work so hard instead of going on a camping trip or on a hiking trip with him. Desi, on the other hand, was furious because she could not understand how Bill could think about fun and trips and vacation when there

Fourth Grade

were all those responsibilities and duties to get out of the way, finished and done. How much more typical can this be? To make the story more complete: Bill worked in the entertainment business while Desi was a school director. Both of them found the work that they felt most comfortable with since their childhood.

A question to ask your child, to understand where they are today:

> Name each sibling by first name and ask your fourth-grader, "How do you play with (name each)? Who decides what you play?"

You can also simply watch the sibling chemistry and try your best to help them get along better.

How to maximize your fourth-grader today:

- Watch the chemistry of the two children playing together and encourage a better interaction from an adult perspective.

- If one bullies (or ignores) the other, help the older or stronger develop empathy for the needs of the younger and weaker by helping the stronger child see the weaker one from a more adult perspective.

- Help the younger or weaker see the older or stronger through more adult eyes well.

Fourth Grade

7. *Age 9 is shaping your child's adult*

RELATIONSHIPS

As a mature adult today looking back on your fourth grade ...

Did you play almost exclusively with boys?
Did you play almost exclusively with girls?
Did you play with both boys and girls?

What are your most comfortable relationships today?

Do you relate most comfortably to men or women today? Or do you relate comfortably to both?

Do you see the parallel between adult comfort zones and your fourth-grade relationships?

Common patterns we have seen with our clients.

1. A question we frequently ask adult men and women is, "In the fourth grade did you play almost exclusively with boys, exclusively with girls, or did you play with both?"

    Boys often played almost exclusively with brothers and boy teammates and almost "spit" at the girls. At the same time, many girls grew up only with brothers and to "survive" on the playground, they learned how to compete and play with boys. These girls rarely related to other girls on the playground.

Fourth Grade

Very frequently, adult men or women who grew up relating exclusively to boys, but did not have anything to do with the girls, relate very effectively to men as adults but feel somewhat (or very) uncomfortable trying to relate to adult women.

2. At the time ...

   Girls often played almost exclusively with sisters and girl teammates and almost "spit" at the boys. At the same time many boys grew up only with sisters. These boys were often far more comfortable on the playground playing with girls. These boys rarely related to other boys on the playground.

   Very frequently, adult men or women who grew up relating exclusively to girls, but did not have anything to do with the boys, relate very effectively to women as adults but feel uncomfortable trying to relate to adult men.

3. Adults who played with both boys and girls as fourth-graders grow up feeling comfortable relating to both men and women. It gives adults an advantage in life if, as fourth-graders, they learn to play comfortably (with mutual respect) with both boys and girls.

Fourth Grade

CASE STUDY — Emőke

When Rhonda was 9 years old, she remembers getting the boys to play Catch Me If You Can; she also remembers organizing the girls during recess to play acrobats in the school bathroom. Her classmates followed her and played with her. She was comfortable with boys and girls and had no difficulty relating to either of them. Rhonda is in her late 40s now and is a coach leading men and women. She is often characterized as the female coach who relates surprisingly well to male leadership problems and understands female leadership struggles in a unique way. **Rhonda's adult comfort zone is exactly the same as it was as a fourth-grader — with both females and males.**

A question to ask your child to understand where they are today:

> Do you play just with boys or with girls, or with both boys and girls?

How to maximize your fourth-grader today:

- Encourage (arrange for) your daughter or son to play with both boys and girls.

- Help them see the reasons to play with both boys and girls, from an adult perspective.

Fourth Grade

- Encourage similar-age family members (e.g., cousins) to get together. (Often it is easier to play with different gender cousins than kids at school.)

8. *Age 9 is shaping your child's adult*

COMPETITIVENESS

As a mature adult today looking back on your fourth grade ...

When you played games did you:

- Have to win, or pout and get angry?
- Want to win, and learn how to do it better next time if you didn't?
- Just enjoy playing the game?

What is your competitive level today?

Do you see the parallel between your competitive drive today and in the fourth grade? Did you have to win, want to win, or just enjoy playing the game in the fourth grade? How do you feel today?

Very common patterns we have seen with our clients.

1. Often husbands and wives differ greatly in this area. Often a husband is extremely competitive and the wife simply enjoys playing the game.

Or the opposite can be true, where the wife is extremely competitive and the husband somewhat enjoys playing the game. Often the couple look at each other like, "Why don't you grow up and do it right?" "Right," of course, means "like I do it!"

2. In the workplace this dimension often shows up very clearly.

    In some situations, the team leader simply wants the team to come together, play together, and work together. One or more of the members can't stop competing with the rest of the team and it simply divides the team. In other situations, the team leader desperately wants competitive team members to compete with the competition and is not looking for a person who simply enjoys playing the game. Understanding the team members' fourth-grade competitive nature is often helpful in recruiting the right team members for any given team.

3. Occasionally on a team you have a situation in which most of the team members are simply enjoying the game, but one of the team members cannot lose as a good sport. Team members do not respect team members who kick their way to the locker room if they lose.

Fourth Grade

CASE STUDY — Emőke

Frank grew up with two sisters and an older brother. He remembers admiring his older brother and wanting to be just like him. He remembers many times when the adults laughed at him as he was trying to win the game and was focusing so hard on winning. He is a competitive spirit who takes part in all possible competitions. He has won a winery contest, swimming competitions, and piano competitions, he has completed the Ironman Triathlon, and he has won several outstanding worker and outstanding achievement awards and he loves every minute of it. **When he talks about a new challenge, his eyes sparkle and he smiles:** "I am going to win this one, I just know it!" And, you guessed it, he wins.

A question to ask your child to understand where they are today:

> When you are playing games, do you have to win or do you just enjoy playing the game? What do you do when you don't win?

How to maximize your fourth-grader today:

- Help them know how to process losing and to learn lessons for the next time.

- Help them win and encourage them to try to win even if they cannot imagine winning; teach them to fight the battle.

Fourth Grade

- Help them play for the fun of the game. Some kids need to learn that winning or losing is part of the game but the real fun is just playing the game.

9. *Age 9 is shaping your child's adult*

FRIENDSHIPS PATTERN

As a mature adult today looking back on your fourth grade ...

What was/were your most comfortable social relationship(s) as a fourth-grader:
- ❍ One best friend?
- ❍ Two or three close friends?
- ❍ Friendly to everyone but close to no one?
- ❍ Loner?
- ❍ With cousins occasionally?
- ❍ Other?

What are your most comfortable social relationships today?

Today, can you see the parallel between your most comfortable social relationships in the fourth grade and today? Typically, if you take a few minutes it becomes very obvious. Either you have a similar relational pattern or you are looking for it.

Fourth Grade

Very common patterns we have seen with our clients:

1. One best friend — who took the lead?

    If a fourth-grader had one best friend, when they become an adult their typically most comfortable social relationship is a deep friendship with one friend.

    If in the fourth grade they led their best friend, today as an adult they tend to lead. If in the fourth grade they were led by their friend, today as an adult they're led by their friend as well.

    This is a very common pattern.

2. Three buddies.

    If a fourth-grader has three close friends, it is predictable they have three close friends today or are emotionally looking for a friend or two to make up a group of four friends like in fourth grade.

    If a person in the fourth grade had three close friends and now has three close friends today, it is very difficult to become part of that group. They have all the friends they need, thank you! But if one of their friends leaves then the foursome is looking for another friend to join the group.

    This is also, a very common pattern!

3. Another very common pattern is the fourth-grader whose family moved a lot.

   The child's family may have been in the military or a parent simply changed jobs frequently. With the family moving a lot, it may have been difficult for the fourth-grader to form deep friendships outside the family. The family often becomes the only trustworthy social connection. The fourth-grader develops deep friendships with siblings but no real deep friendships in the classroom, on the playground, or in the neighborhood.

   Today the adult may have deep continuing relationships with family members and their spouse's family but may not have close friendships outside the family constellation.

   Another very common pattern!

CASE STUDY — Emőke

Linda grew up in a big family and had a wide circle of friends. She remembers going to her friend's house after school and sitting and talking for hours with her friends. As she grew up, she kept her pattern of friendships. Although she moved to a different part of the country she still easily develops new friendships and has several friends. She treasures these friendships and organizes small trips, vacations, dinners and get-togethers where she can regularly meet with them. She says the darkest season of her life was when she

Fourth Grade

was a foreign exchange student abroad; she had a hard time without her friends. **Her comfort zone of friendships is obviously a large circle of friends** and when she cannot have it, she struggles.

A question to ask your child to understand where they are today:

Who are you really good friends with today? Anyone else?

How to maximize your fourth-grader today:

- Arrange or encourage social and relational skills in addition to family members.

- If your child has no friends, work toward helping your child build deeper friendships (invite kids to sleep over, for example).

- Teach your fourth-grader social skills to help build healthy friendships, help them resolve conflicts, use healthy boundaries and celebrate reconciliations.

- Encourage your child to be involved in group activities — sports, church, clubs, etc. — and encourage them to develop friends in the groups.

Fourth Grade

10. *Age 9 is shaping your child's adult*

LIFE ORIENTATION

As a mature adult today looking back on your fourth grade ...

Which of these did your world revolve around in the fourth grade? (alphabetical list)

- Church.
- Dad.
- Family.
- Friends.
- Me.
- Mother.
- School.
- Sports.
- Other ___

What is your most comfortable and relaxed world to be in today?

Take a minute and reflect on where you feel the most relaxed.

Where did you feel the most relaxed, most confident, safest and most accepted in the fourth grade?

Do you see a parallel?

Fourth Grade

Very common patterns we have seen with our clients.

1. How do you orient yourself today as an adult?

In the fourth grade my world revolved around…	Today, my world revolves around …
Church.	Church.
Dad.	Dad.
Family.	Family.
Friends.	Social life.
Me.	Me.
Mother.	Mother.
School.	Work.
Sports.	Sports.
Other.	

2. Mate's orientation

In the fourth grade my spouse's world revolved around…	Today, my spouse's world revolves around …
Church.	Church.
Dad.	Dad.
Family.	Family.
Friends.	Social life.
Me.	Me.
Mother.	Mother.

Fourth Grade

School.	Work.
Sports.	Sports.
Other.	

3. Team members and others' orientations.

   Make a list of your top five friends, teammates, acquaintances.

   How would you say they are oriented today?

   Are they oriented like you are?

   Do they have a very different orientation coming from their fourth grade?

   Does this explain some of the ways in which you are different in major ways?

CASE STUDY — Emőke

When I asked George, a successful businessman and enterpreneur, about his fourth-grade experience, his face lit up. "I was cool! Extremely cool. I was in the center of attention!" Then he was all excited as he described one of his favorite teachers who encouraged him in trying new things. As George described his fourth-grade teacher, he changed into a busy-bee little boy who cannot sit in one place. He talked about his

Fourth Grade

teacher, who gave his time and energy to motivating the young boy to investigate and experiment with the ideas that came into his mind. Today George is a successful businessman surrounded by friends and other businessmen who are asking for his insights and motivation about new businesses and growth possibilities. In the fourth grade, George was most comfortable being cool and being the center of attention. He was most comfortable leading and creating. Today that is exactly what he does. He leads others and creates new businesses while always **being the center of attention.**

A question to ask your child to understand where they are today:

> What's the most important thing in your life today?
>
> What's the most important thing in our family today?

How to maximize your fourth-grader today:

- Ask yourself: What does my child's world actually revolve around today?
  What would I like it to revolve around?
  (Find a way to help it move in that direction)

- Spend time today with your child talking about what you would like your child's mind and heart to revolve around today and form later as an adult.

- If life seems to revolve completely around your child, you may want them to play with a few older children, as they will need to learn to revolve around someone else's agenda.

  It will help them in later life.

D. TAKING ADVANTAGE
   of understanding the fourth-grade
   turning points

1. PARENTS
   Raising a fourth-grader

> A quick overview of this section:
>
> - CAUTION: NO PARENT IS PERFECT!
> - Appreciate what a child does right more than you criticize what they do wrong.
> - Recognize and remember that age 9/fourth grade is the only year of its kind.
> - Give your child unconditional love — the key to "LIFE CONFIDENCE."
> - Give a "HEART NAME" to every fourth-grader you care about personally.
> - Look for natural strength or unique strength.
> - Give each child five to 10 positive adjectives you call her or him over and over.
> - Watch carefully who your child considers "good friends."
> - Teach your child to make and manage money.
> - Encourage your child to play with boys and girls.
> - Help your child be in situations where they are called on to both lead and follow.
> - Warning: Never tell your fourth-grade son to "take care of Mama while Daddy is gone"!

CAUTION: NO PARENT IS PERFECT

Do not be overwhelmed by feeling you have to do all of these perfectly all the time. These are just a few thoughts you may want to look at and consider.

Chances are, you are already doing most of these.

Consider starting with just one action that is needed at this moment and when you feel it has been accomplished, move on to another.

Remember: NO PARENT IS A PERFECT PARENT — WE ALL MAKE MISTAKES! Our genuine unconditional love for our children does help cover a multitude of mistakes!

Below you will find a few of the keys we have found helpful in talking with thousands of parents and clients who were once fourth-graders.

Appreciate what a child does right more than you criticize what they do wrong.

As you look back on the last week, have more of your comments addressed what your fourth-grader has done right or what your fourth-grader needs to improve or has done wrong?

Whatever he or she does right and you appreciate, you'll see more of.

Fourth Grade

If you tell them what they did wrong in pitching the ball, they will want to stop trying to pitch ball at all. Focus on what your fourth-grader does right, not on what they need to improve — not what they have done wrong!

If your fourth-grader pitches the ball right and you tell them they pitched the ball right, they will pitch a ball right more in the future.

Recognize and remember that age 9/fourth grade is the only year of its kind.

It is the one year you have to most dramatically shape your child's comfort zones.

You can adjust them a little bit before and after, but fourth grade is one unique year.

Give your child unconditional love — the key to "LIFE CONFIDENCE."

"Life confidence" in a person develops (or does not develop) before the child goes to school. If children feel parents love them without condition, they go to school with life confidence. They know that their parents will still love them even if they do not perform their schoolwork perfectly.

Life is OK — confidence! Life feels secure. Life feels safe. Life feels OK!

However, those children who sense no love, conditional love or inconsistent love at home have to wear a mask of false confidence when they go to school.

To them, life is not OK, but they put on an emotional mask so others do not see they are uncertain and afraid. They develop situational confidence — i.e., they are confident in certain situations but feel generally insecure in the rest of life.

A child who receives inconsistent or conditional love may feel he or she has to perform to get love, or may feel he or she cannot depend on being loved. Tell children you love them, especially at age 9/fourth grade! Children are not good guessers. They assume a lot, frequently building an adult lifestyle based on false assumptions from the fourth grade. Do not make children guess whether you love them or not. We are not just talking about your own children but also your grandchildren, your nieces and/or nephews — every child you genuinely care about.

Give a "HEART NAME" to every fourth-grader you care about personally.

A "heart name" is a name only you call only her or him, only when you are alone.

Fourth Grade

We all have three selves:
   a public self everybody sees,
   a private self only close friends and
      relatives see, and
   a personal self only we have ever seen.

Our personal self is what is called your heart. Remember the Bible verse:
   "As a man thinketh in his heart so is he."

When you are alone with a fourth-grader, and you say, "Honey bun, that isn't the way you do it," he or she thinks you are talking directly to her or his heart. It is not a mental connection, it is a heart connection.

The child thinks, "Dad or Mom only calls me 'honey bun.' Dad or Mom must be talking to the real me."

When that child gets to be 16, 17, 18 years old, and he or she comes in with a blue Mohawk haircut, when you're alone together you can still say, "Honey bun…" You will be right back in your child's heart.

You would be surprised at the number of adults who never had a heart name and can never remember even being called by their first name. All they can remember is hearing, "Kids, come to dinner," or "Kids, be quiet, or I'm coming up there," or "Kids, get in the car, it's time to go!" These adults can never remember actually being seen as a person as a child, let alone as a very special child. They remember feeling like they were "part of the herd." Give any child you care anything about a heart name!

Look for natural strength or unique strength.

No matter how many children you have, see each one as a unique little person in the process of becoming a unique adult person, not just one of the herd.

Give each child five to 10 positive adjectives you call her or him over and over.

Your self-concept is the sum total of all of the adjectives you use to describe yourself — to yourself. Unfortunately, the negative adjectives you use to describe a child will stay with them for life. Fortunately, so will the positive ones.

Look for natural strengths your child actually has and turn them into positive adjectives. Keep repeating these adjectives; they will become a permanent part of your child's adult self-concept.

Watch carefully who your child considers "good friends."

You have heard the saying "Be careful the friends

Fourth Grade

you choose, for you will become like them!" Make sure your child gets time with the children you want your child to become more like and less time with those you do not want your child to be more like.

Allow your child to have sleepovers. A parent once told me he would not let his kids sleep over at friends' houses because he could not be sure what the kids would do. Fine. Let other kids come over to your place to sleep over. Sleepovers are where children learn how to become more than just playground friends. They get beyond what they see in school and share secrets. Sleepovers let them know how to relate in a heart-to-heart conversation. If a child is allowed to have sleepovers, it will be far easier to relate at a deeper adult level.

If you realize your child spends much more time with adults than with other children, or that he or she is always with kids and is never with adults, try to help the child find balance in these relationships.

Teach your child to make and manage money.

Many parents provide everything for their children until their teen years and beyond because they can easily afford to do so. RED LIGHT! When the child today becomes an adult tomorrow, they will have a very limited understanding of the value of a dollar. They may well grow up thinking, "Someone will take care of me": Mom and Dad, a spouse, the government, etc. They may have an attitude of entitlement toward life and may not really understand the value of hard work and its relationship to life.

Encourage your child to play with boys and girls.

If they play with both boys and girls in the fourth grade, they will relate far more comfortably to men and women as an adult. And your child's husband or wife will appreciate the comfort of their relationship for decades.

Help your child be in situations where they are called on to both lead and follow.

If you have an older child and a younger child, and one is always the leader and one is always the follower, at times separate the kids in the fourth grade. Put your leader child in situations with older kids so that the boy or girl has to follow. And let the one who is always following be with younger kids so he or she gets to lead. Ideally, as an adult they need to be able to lead when it is appropriate and follow when it is appropriate.

Fourth Grade

WARNING: Never tell your fourth-grade son to "take care of Mama while Daddy is gone"!

One very common thing fathers say to fourth-grade sons while leaving on a trip is "Daddy has to go on a business trip, take care of Mama." No! No fourth-grade boy feels adequate enough to really "take care of Mama." He will nod his head as if to say, "Yes." But in his heart he is now old enough to know he can't. He is asking himself all the time you are gone, "What if something goes wrong? I see how that strange man is looking at Mama — am I supposed to hit him or something? What if a burglar tries to get in the house — can I really take care of her?" He is old enough to see and know what "taking care of Mama" may mean, but he is just as sure he may not be able to if the actual time comes where he needs to do something.

Instead say, "Daddy is going to be gone for a while but Mama is here to take care of you. Now be a good and helpful boy for Mama, OK?" A nod means a fourth-grade-level promise but without fourth-grade pressure! Don't put adult responsibilities on your fourth-grader; allow him/her to be a child with responsibilities of a child only and nothing more.

2. AUNTS, UNCLES, GRANDPARENTS
Helping parents raise a fourth-grader

> A quick overview of this section:
>
> - Be aware of the values you are teaching.
> - Be a cheerleader, not a critic.
> - See each child's unique heart.
> - Tell family stories.
> - Have fun!

Be aware of the values you are teaching.

Who are you closest to, your mother or your father? Who loved you the most as a fourth-grader? Perhaps it wasn't either of your parents. Was it your grandma, your grandpa, aunt, or uncle?

Picture that person in your mind. When you were in the fourth grade, what were the three most important things to this person? What were their three highest values? They may have put those values into words, but their or his actions modeled those values for you. This person may never have said, "Look, you need to drive a Buick," but every Saturday you would see him polishing the chrome circles on the Buick's fenders!

When you were in the fourth grade, what were the three most important things to this person?

Fourth Grade

Give yourself time to think about this. Write them down here:

1.

2.

3.

Now ask yourself, "How important are these values to me today?"

Many adults are surprised to find how much their aunt's, uncle's or grandparent's values, even unspoken, have influenced them as adults. Now think about your own aunts, uncles, or grandparents.

Fourth-graders intuitively pick up what is important to you, just as you absorbed some of your primary values from your family relatives.

If your grandchildren, nieces, or nephews just watch you without ever listening to your words, what are they going to value for the rest of their lives?

Be a cheerleader, not a critic.

At this point in your adult life, you are probably a very analytical person. It is easy for you to put on your "analytical hat" and see what is wrong with your fourth-grader. Perhaps he or she is holding the bat wrong. Perhaps he or she is holding the pencil wrong. You know your child would be more successful if he or she just listened to you and adjusted a few things.

But your fourth-graders often need cheerleaders even more than they need constructive criticism. Use your analytical skill to find what they are doing right instead of what they are doing wrong. It is easy to correct but keep a balance in correcting and supporting your child. Choose your battles and be wise! Be their cheerleader!

See each child's unique heart.

No matter how many children you have at the family picnic, see each one as a unique little person in the process of becoming a unique adult person, not just one of many grandchildren, nieces or nephews.

Tell family stories.

Children love to hear family stories of the "old days." Give your children a deep sense of roots with stories of your great-grandparents; go back as far as you can remember, and also share stories you have read about family history. Show them family antiques and tell any stories you know connected to the items. Tell them stories about

Fourth Grade

your grandparents, your parents, your own life growing up — good times and bad — your children (their parents), and your love for them!

Children love to be read to.
Read material that you think will positively shape their values and thoughts for a lifetime.

Show them family pictures, albums, and bring them the stories of their ancestors. One of the most important core longings of humans is the desire to belong. By telling them stories about their family, by giving them roots in their family, you actually help them belong, which will secure their identity for their adult life.

Help your grandchildren, nieces and nephews feel
　you belong here,
　you are part of us,
　you are an important part of this family!

Have fun!

All too often, parents at this phase of life are under so much pressure, there is not a lot of time left for uninhibited, spontaneous FUN!
This is a role you can play ... have FUN!

3. CLERGY, COACHES, EDUCATORS
Helping parents raise fourth-graders

> A quick overview of this section:
>
> - Adult comfort zones are being shaped in your care today.
> - Your very best staff need to be at the fourth-grade level.
> - Focus on each child's uniqueness, strength and positive adjectives.
> - You are a model of what your fourth-grader (in part) will become.
> - Teach each of your students to both lead and follow — in your field.

Let me ask you one simple question:

What if it were absolutely proven that fourth grade is the single most shaping point in a child's life? What would you do differently?

Let's look now at the fourth grade and adult comfort zones, seeing specific implications for your role as children's workers, clergy, coaches and educators.

Adult comfort zones are being shaped in your care today.

Every organization is a direct reflection of its

Fourth Grade

leadership. The organization reflects both the leader's strengths and the leader's weaknesses. Your entire organization is a direct reflection of you. The longer you are in place, the more direct the reflection is.

You are responsible for the leaders placed at the fourth-grade level today. You are, in fact, responsible for the fourth-graders under your care. Make absolutely sure the fourth-graders are well taken care of today.

What they experienced today in your organization is what they will remember emotionally as adults. If they have a positive experience today, they will see your organization and organizations like yours in a positive light in their adult years. If they experience your organization negatively today, they will see your organization and organizations like yours in a very negative light in their adult years.

Protect your fourth-grader's experiences in your organization today!

Your very best staff need to be at the fourth-grade level.

If you are professionally responsible for children, pay very close attention to who is teaching and caring for your fourth-graders. If you have a teacher who is mean-spirited or not loving, reassign or release that teacher immediately! Get that teacher out of the classroom. I do not care if he or she has been there 50 years. That teacher is shaping your children's view of the future of your institution. You do not have to worry as much about the teachers of other grade levels, but do not have a bad teacher teaching fourth-graders. Your finest educators need to be in the fourth grade shaping your children.

Focus on each child's uniqueness, strength and positive adjectives.

Remember, your self-concept is the sum total of all of the adjectives you use to describe yourself, to yourself.

Unfortunately, the negative adjectives you use to describe a child will stay with them for life. Fortunately, so will the positive ones.

Look for natural strengths your fourth-grade child actually has and turn them into positive adjectives. Keep repeating these adjectives — they become a permanent part of your child's self-concept. Keep looking for and focus on what they are doing right, not what they are doing wrong.

Focus on their strengths and help them see that many of their "weaknesses" will actually be irrelevant as adults.

Fourth Grade

You are a model of what your fourth-grader (in part) will become.

As your fourth-graders watch you today, what do they see?

You are modeling for them what adults are supposed to be like. They will in fact be like you as an adult. Be very careful what you are modeling for these impressionable young minds and hearts.

You are one of their adult models!

Teach each of your students to both lead and follow — in your field.

Under your care, your fourth-graders today are learning their role within your institution in their adult years.

Would you prefer that all of your students be leaders? Would you prefer that all of your students be followers? Or, would you prefer that all of your students become both leaders and followers? Look carefully at each child to see their potential as an adult, and help them grow into that potential as fourth-graders under your care.

Fourth Grade

SPECIAL NOTE:

Were you a "teacher's pet"?

Often an adult is embarrassed to admit, "I was 'teacher's pet,'" because they remember the lack of respect other kids had for the teacher's pet in the fourth grade.

A teacher's pet is typically a child who is very smart, very articulate, and related mostly to adults at home before they went to school. So when they got to school, they already knew how to relate to adult teachers better than they knew how to relate to the other kids. Most of their peers did not know how to relate to the teacher; they were just playing with each other.

The teacher's pet understands what the teacher wants. Teachers' pets do what the teacher wants.

The teacher likes them, so they are given special privileges and more responsibility than the other children.

About 20 percent of participants in the leadership groups I work with say they were a teacher's pet growing up. If you are a leader or educator today, chances are you were a teacher's pet.

If you were a teacher's pet, you may find this interesting. If you were a teacher's pet, your friends today are typically 10 years older than you because

Fourth Grade

you are still more comfortable relating to older people than you are relating to your peers. *Right?*

(So far, about 100 percent of the teacher's pets have smiled and answered, "RIGHT!")

4. TODAY
Fourth-grade implications for dating and marriage

> A quick overview of this section:
>
> - Your life orientation and your possible mate's life orientation.
> - Your gender relationships and possible mate's gender relationships.
> - Your life values and your possible mate's life values.
> - Your community commitments and your possible mate's community commitments.
> - Would you have played together on the fourth-grade playground?

In the first five to 10 years of a marriage, husband and wife are often unconsciously or secretly asking,

- Is my way of looking at life right, or is her/his way of looking at life right?

- Was my family right or was her/his family right?

- Am I stronger or is he/she stronger?

- Why doesn't he/she grow up and do it the right way — like my family did?

That is not the way to live life. The question is not "Am I right or are you right?" The question is:

- How are we different and how do we best work and fit together?

Some of those answers come from your fourth-grade experiences.

It is important to understand how your spouse is different from you and what differing assumptions he or she grew up with at home. Perhaps your family had people over all the time socializing, but your spouse's family never had anyone over. You say, "We never have anyone over." Your spouse responds, "What do you mean? We had someone over just last year." It is OK to be different as adults. You do not have to be the same, but it is very helpful to understand where and why you are different.

Take the 10 comfort zones described in Section C of this book and ask your fiancé or spouse about their experiences in the fourth grade. This is a great exercise to get to know and understand each other at a much deeper level.

Fourth Grade

See how each point or question below has specific implications for your dating or marriage relationship.

Your life orientation and your possible mate's life orientation.

IN THE FOURTH GRADE:
- What or who did your world revolve around?

TODAY:
- What or who does or should our world revolve around?

Your gender relationships and your possible mate's most comfortable gender relationships.

IN THE FOURTH GRADE:
- Who did you mostly playwith: boys, girls, or both?
- Would we have played together on the fourth-grade playground?
- Why?
- Why not?

TODAY:
- Who are you most comfortable with: men, women, or both?
- How would you rate our natural compatibility today?
- How can we improve it in any way?

Fourth Grade

Your life values and your possible mate's life values.

1. Draw two circles.
2. Each person, without looking at the other's circle, divides the circle into pie-slice shapes according to the percentage of time spent (in the fourth grade) in the following categories:
    - Alone.
    - Church.
    - Family time.
    - School or studying for school.
    - Socializing.
    - With extended family.
    - Working.
    - Other.

Now, compare circles. Do you see where your tensions may be today? One couple Bobb consulted with saw their tensions immediately. She spent about 40 percent of her time socializing in the fourth grade. He spent 50 percent of his time in school or studying for school and 50 percent with his family — zero socializing. Today, as adults, she wants to socialize with friends a lot. He sees and feels no need for any kind of socializing.

Can you predict one of the obvious tension spots in their marriage — or in yours?

Fourth Grade

Your community commitments and your possible mate's community commitments.

Discuss all of your activities outside of the classroom and family activities as a fourth-grader. Discuss your role in the activity. How did the activity make you feel? How do you think this activity has affected your adult comfort zones and values?

Would you have played together on the fourth-grade playground?

Another question you may find fascinating is to ask each other, "Would we have played together in the fourth grade?"

Often this question and its imagined answer points out very quickly where the tension is an adult relationship.

We hope the above discussions have led to some very interesting conversations and some much deeper insights into your date, fiancé or spouse.

5. TODAY
Fourth-grade implications for *building a strong team*

> A quick overview of this section:
>
> - Fourth grade makes life surprisingly predictable.
> - Clearly defined life values.
> - Your adult comfort in relating to men and women.
> - Level of leadership — not everyone wants to be president!
> - Your adult leadership patterns.
> - Entrepreneurial comfort level.
> - Your adult social patterns.

Fourth grade makes life surprisingly predictable.

BOBB: I am a presidential mentor/consultant. Over the past 40-plus years I have spent more than 50,000 hours behind the defenses of some of the finest leaders of our generation. Spending time with the senior executive, the senior executive couple, or an executive team — and asking endless questions — is my work and responsibility.

Fourth Grade

MY CONCLUSION:

Our adult comfort zones, even at the very senior executive level, are a reflection of what happened in the fourth grade.

And they are, fortunately, extremely helpful in predicting team chemistry and building a strong long-term team.

You may have heard the expression, "The best time to fire a person is when you don't hire her or him."

But the trick in building a strong team is trying to see who the person really is and how they will actually function on your team.

Before you hire someone, it is ideal to get a good feel for who will fit and who will eventually
    polarize the team,
    try to take over or dominate the team,
    never want to lead the team,
    just be happy to be a part of the team,
    or not get along with men or women.

When you are recruiting for a position and you want to get behind the smile, ask about the fourth grade.

I like to start an interview looking all formal and ready to fill out the official paperwork. Then with an obvious (but casual) tossing down of my

Fourth Grade

pen, I lean back in my chair and say, "Look, before we get started with the more formal part of the interview, let me ask you a few questions. Where did you grow up as a kid? Let's say the fourth grade. Where did you live at that time? What role did you play on the playground? At that time did you care more what the teachers thought than your little friends, or care more what your little friends thought than the teachers?" In a relaxed, very comfortable style, we chat our way through the 10 comfort zones in light of her or his fourth-grade experience.

Often the interview is over before filling out the paperwork because I can see that this person's comfort zones will not match the need our organization has today.

A quick example: If you were hiring a vice president to move to Chicago and open a whole new division for your organization, you would need someone who is aggressive, social, organized, and who would make it happen. You interview two people. They both have MBA degrees from equally exceptional Ivy League graduate schools. They both graduated at the head of their class. They both have strong computer skills. They have the smile. They have the image, the package, everything. You cannot tell which would be a better choice. You actually like them both equally!

Then you ask about the fourth grade.

Fourth Grade

>One says, "I was a loner. I played alone most of the time with my computer."
>
>The other candidate is the one that knocked on doors, organized teams, and "always won"!
>
>What do you think will happen when your new VP gets to Chicago and hears his 13th "NO!" in a row?
>
>One is going to want to retreat to the safety of their hotel room. The other one is going to go out and meet some more people. Your hiring decision becomes crystal clear after gaining just a few insights from the fourth grade.

For a few minutes let's go back through the adult comfort zones and see how each one has specific implications for your role as a leader of any organization, business or team.

Clearly defined life values

>Whenever hiring an executive-level leader, carefully check to see if the person's life values are in alignment with the organization's core values. You can typically find this alignment, or lack of it, by simply asking what they value.
>
>However, when a person really wants a position, he or she may shade their answers a bit to seem more in alignment with what they know to be the

Fourth Grade

core values of the organization. When you are wanting to go a bit deeper here is what you ask:

Let's go back for a minute to your fourth grade, when you were 9 years old.

Where did you grow up?
_____

What was your father's first name?
_____

What was his occupation?
_____

As you watched (use father's first name) _____, what three things were the most important things to him at that time?

1. _____

2. _____

3. _____

What was your mother's first name?
_____

What was her occupation?
_____

Fourth Grade

As you watched (use mother's first name) _____, what three things were the most important things to her at that time?

1. _____

2. _____

3. _____

Typically, the six things listed above are today extremely important to your candidate.

If these six things were extremely important values to your candidate, would they be in alignment with the values you want your candidate to have today? If not, you need to at least explore these areas carefully before hiring this candidate. If you are interviewing two candidates, which one has these six values and is closest to the values you are looking for in this position?

We always (at least initially) assume the above six values have been passed down to the person we are interviewing!

Fourth Grade

Your adult comfort in relating to men and women.

DO NOT
have a man (or woman) who related almost exclusively
to boys in the fourth grade
try to lead a division of women.

DO NOT
have a woman (or man) who related almost exclusively to girls in the fourth grade
lead a division of men.

Level of leadership — not everyone wants to be president!

There are actually two reasons people want to be president of an organization.

1. They were leading nearly everything they were involved in during their fourth grade.
They want to control so they can lead effectively.

2. They were leading nearly nothing in their fourth grade.
They want to be president so they can be in control.
They want to lead so they are never out of control.

Many top-level leaders are seen by all of their peers as presidential material. They are often asked to be the senior leader, president, CEO, executive director, senior pastor, etc. However, when they were in the fourth grade they never led the playground. They were always first chosen. As adults, their preferred, adult comfort zone, most desired position is the senior vice president — never the president! If appointed or elected to the top position it puts a great deal of pressure on the person and it is typically not long before they seek a position where they are no longer the senior executive!

Your adult leadership patterns.

Can you find a natural alignment between a comfortable role this candidate played in the fourth grade and the role you will be asking her or him to play in your organization?

If not, be careful! When exhausted, he or she will tend to revert to their natural comfort zones.

Another problem: If you are asking this person to lead people they could not have led on the fourth-grade playground, it rarely works well!

To overdramatize and oversimplify a point, be very careful when asking the fourth-grade playground loner who is now an adult to lead the fourth-grade football team, also now adults.

Eventually, the fourth-grade social chemistry will likely take over.

Fourth Grade

One of the interesting patterns I've seen over and over again:

If you were **a leader on the playground**, chances are much higher that you will feel more comfortable in a larger, existing firm — i.e., in an environment where you adjust to "playing with" and leading the people who are already there.

If you were not the leader on the playground but were **the leader in the neighborhood** after school where you got to decide who you would go play with, chances are you are far more comfortable starting your own entrepreneurial enterprise as an adult, an environment where you can choose who you will play with and lead.

Entrepreneurial comfort level

Discomfort

> Many of my clients make a great deal of money, but they never feel comfortable with it. They grew up feeling poor. They are not comfortable with their wealth. Oh, most would like to have lots of money, but actually never feel really comfortable in a world of wealth. There is a feeling of "I really don't fit here."
>
> Other clients, today in ministry, grew up feeling rich. Today as adults, as dedicated as they are, they struggle with the feeling of being "poor" in

Fourth Grade

the ministry and not having money. There is a feeling of "I really don't fit here."

Others, who grew up feeling in between, experience discomfort being either rich or poor as adults. There is a feeling of "I really don't fit here."

No one is really comfortable in a financial world that is very different from the financial world in which they grew up as a fourth-grader.

Comfort

On the other hand:
If you grew up feeling rich, and you are rich as an adult, you feel, "Of course, this is as it is supposed to be."

If you grew up feeling in between, and you are neither rich nor poor as an adult, you feel, "Of course, this is as it is supposed to be" — even when your dreams include being rich one day.

If you grew up feeling poor, and you are poor as an adult, you feel, "Of course, this is as it is supposed to be" — even when your dreams include being rich one day.

Is there alignment with this position and the candidate's fourth-grade feelings?

Your adult social patterns.

In the fourth grade, were you most comfortable relating to adults or to your peers?

If you answered "my peers," you typically care more what your colleagues say and think than you do what the president, manager or boss does.

If you answered "adults," you typically care more what the president, manager or boss wants done even if the team doesn't.

6. TODAY
Overcoming a traumatic fourth grade

A quick overview of this section:

- Looking at the fourth grade from an adult perspective.
- Calling your parents by their first names.
- Defining a life dream pulling you into a positive future.
- Building a life milestone list and never comparing yourself with anyone!
- Warning: Don't be shocked if you find yourself returning to your comfort zones when you're feeling exhausted or pressured in other ways.

Fourth Grade

You may be asking, "What if my fourth grade wasn't an ideal experience?"

Susan came to me struggling with anxiety about being sick and a fear of death. Even before I asked her about her past experiences with sickness or death, she started talking about her fourth-grade years. When she was in fourth grade one of her classmates died in an accident, and she also saw another classmate choking in class. In both cases she was not supported by others and was not asked about her feelings and thoughts, but was left alone with her thoughts and fear. She often wished somebody would have asked her about what she was feeling, but she has no memory of getting attention of any sort. Today her most intense fear is choking and other throat problems and a **fear of death**. She still struggles with the feeling that **people don't pay enough attention to her.**

Fortunately and unfortunately, we've discussed this question with literally hundreds of individuals wrestling with a troubled traumatic past and hundreds of parents seeking to "undo the damage" one or more of their children experienced at the tender, vulnerable, life-shaping age of 9.

If you are wrestling with these questions deep in your heart, here are the five best bits of advice we have to give at this point in our life experience.

Fourth Grade

Look at the fourth grade from an adult perspective.

We have found that one of the very best ways to help deal with a trauma in the past is to ask something like this:

Today as a mature adult, how do you see what happened to you as a child? Only use first names: only call your parents by their first names, only call aunts and uncles by their first names, only call teachers by their first names.

Then ask, "If that happened to another child today, how would you see it?"

Often, processing the trauma as though it happened to someone else gives an objectivity to the trauma, the people, and the pain that lets the person begin to see the entire situation with "adult eyes"— not the eyes of an abused, traumatized, perhaps molested child.

Often, calling the key people by their first names allows the abused to see the abuser as also abused. It allows the victim to see the victimizer also as a victim.

Often, this allows the person you are helping resolve part of the trauma of a childhood abuse.

Fourth Grade

Call your parents by their first names.

Here is an insight that has freed a wide variety of people from negative anger, resentment, and even hatred toward their parents and turned it into positive understanding and compassion.

What was your dad's first name?   Write it out here: _____.

What was your mom's first name? Write it out here: _____.

If you have a great relationship with your parents you can skip this exercise. But if you have a less than perfect relationship with your parents, here is our advice:

- In your mind stop calling them "Mom and Dad" or "Mama and Daddy." Call them only by their first names as you are thinking about some of the unwise things they said or did when you were a child! (When you are with them personally, call them what you always have.)
- When you are discussing your parents with a friend, counselor or spouse in private, always call them by their first name!
- If they have passed away, write a letter to them starting with their first names!

Can you feel the difference?

Fourth Grade

No, wait — can you feel the difference as you think of your parents by their first names? Some feel like laughing; others get teary and weep!

Can you feel the difference?

Why call your parents by their first names? It turns them from positions into people, from the position of parent to the person with a first name.

When we see our parents as people — sometimes for the first time — it is a great relief. It instantly and permanently adjusts our expectations of them. We may expect "Mommy and Daddy" to be perfect. To do it perfectly. To say it perfectly. But the young kids who were raising us in the fourth grade were going through a lot of pressures we never understood while growing up. They may have been little more than children raising children. They were dealing with their own unresolved relationships with their parents and their fourth-grade traumas at the hands of imbalanced adults and insensitive playground bullies.

If you feel that unwise, insensitive, even cruel parents victimized you, you may also want to do a very careful study of your grandparents. Your parents may well have been the victims of your grandparents. Understanding where your pain comes from doesn't completely take it away, but it can often make it far less painful. And it gives you "new eyes" to see your parents more as victims

Fourth Grade

than as victimizers.

Many of my clients have testified that it was a major relief the instant they thought of their parents by their first names the very first time.

Define a life dream pulling you into a positive future.

BOBB: In my books *Dream Energy* and *Dreaming Big*, I define a life dream as the difference you hope to make sometime before you die. Having a clear life dream gives you something to run to — to focus on in your future. Without a life dream pulling you into the future you are stuck with running from something: your past!

One principle you can count on: Without an answer to the question "Why," the price of change is always too high.

Your life dream helps answer the questions: Why even try to grow? Why change? Why move toward the future and not be so bound by the pains (such as comments of unthinking people) of the past? A life dream is encouraging. It gives you hope!

Define a life dream that is in alignment with your single greatest strength. Focus on maximizing your strengths and making your weaknesses irrelevant. No one, not even all of the boogeymen and bullies from your past, is good at everything!

Fourth Grade

Based on your life dream, develop a plan to grow into your full, lifelong potential. Also develop a plan to peak in 10 years — and every year on your birthday, move the date out a year. Make a list of your current self-descriptive adjectives forming your self-concept and, one by one, turn your negative adjectives to positive. Grow into your potential as you pursue your life dream!

You may push back a bit: "I'm an adult. Can I change my comfort zones?" Frankly, you can attempt to change your comfort zones, but it will likely take years to do it, and even then, I am not sure you can totally get it done.

At one point in my life I started trying to change three deeply rooted habits or comfort zones:
- To smile more.
- To be more expressive with my voice and not use a monotone.
- To talk faster when speaking in public.

It took me 15 years to change my fourth-grade, comfortable communications style. And yes, frankly, when I'm really exhausted I still want to go flat-faced, smiling at no one!

One day my wife said to me, "Bobb, when you are speaking in public you need to talk faster. You are going to put people to sleep." So I doubled my speed. I told her as fast as I could talk, "Now I sound like a TV pitchman selling cleaning compounds." She said, "Bobb, you are not even up to half the speed most people talk and certainly are not talking as fast as people listen. Double your speed again." So today, you may think I still sound like a person with a very slow drawl, but you should have heard me before I started to speed up.

It took me 15 years of consciously trying to grow in these three areas and it is still an ongoing, conscious effort and focus. One does not typically move from one comfort zone to another overnight. And as I've said, when exhausted we tend to want to return to our fourth-grade comfort zones.

But having a life dream that pulls you into the future makes the frustration of change worth the effort!

Build a life milestone list and never compare yourself with anyone!

One of the lessons we often teach is "Nothing motivates like results!" One of the keys to helping a person with a lot of trauma in the past is to look at all of the results they have actually seen in the past. Have them list all of their life-shaping events, starting with pre-teens, then teens, 20s, 30s, etc. Then have them look at all of the positive milestones they have accomplished. Then have them look at all of the negative things that have happened and all of the lessons they have learned in life as a result of the negative things

Fourth Grade

that they have made their way through.

A second lesson we have taught often is "Never compare yourself with anyone!" Often, a person begins to feel down, discouraged and depressed when they begin comparing themselves to a successful brother, sister, cousin, or classmate. Have the person focus totally on their own progress and on their own hopes for their own future.

Don't be shocked if you find yourself returning to your adult comfort zones when you're feeling exhausted or pressured in other ways.

Our adult comfort zones are where we go to rest from the pressures of the day. When we are feeling tired or fatigued, we all revert to our comfort zones. When you take a few minutes to reflect on where you actually go when you are exhausted, you will find that you tend to go back to the comfort zones you established, for whatever reasons, when you were age 9, most likely in your fourth grade.

Fourth Grade

E. QUESTIONS AND ANSWERS

A few of the common questions we've been asked about the age 9/fourth-grade experience

> ## QUESTION 1.
>
> *What part do heredity and environment play in how we act and react as adults?*

The Bible has an interesting verse, Matthew 19:12. In the New International Version, it reads:
> *For some are eunuchs because they were born that way; others were made that way by men; and others have renounced marriage because of the kingdom of heaven. The one who can accept this should accept it.*

Jesus says that some are eunuchs because God made them that way. Part of who you are is your heredity.

Some eunuchs are eunuchs because man made them that way. Part of what you are is because of your environment, how circumstances or people have shaped you.

Some eunuchs are eunuchs because they decided to be that way for the sake of the gospel. Part of what you are is a result of your own decisions.

We can see from this verse that we are who we are partly from heredity, partly from environment, and partly from our own decisions. Our experience has

Fourth Grade

convinced us your environment in the fourth grade has had a unique and special influence.

> **QUESTION 2.**
>
> *What is the impact of physical stature on the fourth-grade experience?*
>
> *My son is actually the youngest in his class and he's the smallest in his class, even smaller than the girls. I think that really gives him a problem with confidence. It factors into some of the things that happen on the playground. He isn't big enough to participate in sports with the other guys as well as he would like. He had just turned 5 when he started kindergarten. How can I as a parent maybe offset some of those situations?*

Make sure he gets to play with kids in your neighborhood who are smaller than he is, so he gets to experience being one of the bigger kids. Let him learn how to lead the smaller kids as well as to follow the bigger kids.

Help him see he can excel in other areas. He may excel in the classroom or he may excel in some sport that's not a team sport. He may be able to play golf at this point already. He may be a great swimmer or do well in some other sport that doesn't require size to compete.

Fourth Grade

You may want to consider the possibility of keeping him back a year. If he could develop a really good friendship with a third-grader about his size, he may not mind staying back with that friend as opposed to going on with his class.

He is old enough to have an almost adult conversation at a level most adults don't realize. If you were to sit down and talk to him, you would be amazed how much he can pick up about what's really happening to him. Say, "Bobby, you know we thought it was the right idea to start you early, but because you're early you're the smallest in your class and you know what? It makes you feel like you are sort of on the losing end of things all the time. You're really the age of the third-graders." Try to help him see it as you see it as an adult. It may have never occurred to him. He may feel as though he just can't compete with those people, the monsters they call fourth-graders. Help him to see it the way you see it. He may be able to absorb your adult perspective at an amazing level.

Consider talking to your educators about holding him back a year. Even though he can compete academically, it's not just about academics. There is a whole series of things he'll do late. He'll get his driver's license late. He'll start dating late. Throughout junior high and high school, he would be the youngest and the smallest, and at this age, there is still time to adjust a little bit.

Discuss it with your spouse, discuss it with him, discuss it with a wise educator. Holding your child back may not be what you decide to do, but don't rule it out.

> **QUESTION 3.**
>
> *I'm a social worker, and I work with children who are abused and neglected. Specifically, what should I keep in mind?*

BOBB: I work with many executives, many of whom are presidents of organizations, and their spouses. In that intimate three-way conversation, it often comes up that the wife or the husband was sexually or physically abused as a child. I discovered something interesting: The children who process an abusive experience with a healthy adult in a healthy way tend to heal. But children who don't process abuse properly by themselves continue to have problems with that experience.

For example, if you are counseling an adult who was physically molested as a child, if they had an adult who cared about them sit down and explain why it happened, they have a better chance of properly processing the abuse. Explain the bad things that have happened to a fourth-grader in nearly adult logic. He or she is old enough to come to the proper conclusions. It's harder for a first-grader to really process anything seriously, but a fourth-grader is old enough to understand when you say, "It wasn't you.

Fourth Grade

You didn't do anything wrong. It was a bad person that did it to you. You weren't the bad person." Listen to the child's heart and try to help them understand the situation as you (an adult) understand it.

You'll find that if the experience is processed properly, in adulthood the person can remember the abuse, but it's like a scar. If it's not processed in a healthy way, if you assume, "Oh, that's just a child thing, I don't want to upset them anymore," or you just ignore the event or situation, it remains a sore instead of a scar. I've talked to people in their 80s who still have sores from childhood. You ask one question, it hits one of those sores, and they start to weep like little children. Open, painful wounds tend not to dissipate over the years.

If I were a social worker, I would encourage the parent to help the child process and discuss the abuse. The heart name is important here. Remember that the heart name is what you call only her or him, and only when the two of you are alone.

If the parents are the abusers, then another caring adult (e.g., a grandparent, aunt or uncle) needs to step into that gap to help the child process.

Let me tell you a true story. It isn't of a fourth-grader, but it makes my point. My wife Cheryl and I were with another couple and it turned out that their daughter, who was 16, had just been date raped. She went out with this boy. She had just returned home from school when he raped her, and she went into a cocoon, a shell. She wouldn't talk to anybody, including her parents! We were talking with the couple about one week past the trauma and they sobbed, "What do we do to help her? She won't talk to us. She just sits in the corner in a fetal position. She won't open up to anyone." I explained the concept of "heart name" and asked, "What was her heart name as a little girl?" To protect their privacy, let's say they said, "Bunny."

I said, "You're going to have to wait for the right time. The right time is when you're rested enough to really listen and you are ready to talk for a long time — when she feels as safe as you can help her feel. It may be a week, two weeks, three weeks, a month, two months from now, but when you feel the time is right. When she's comfortable, you have plenty of time, and you're safe — just the three of you — ask her one specific gentle question. Just ask, 'Bunny, how are you?' Now be prepared because she's going to weep for a long time."

We asked them to let us know how it turned out. The father called a few weeks later. He said, "Last night it happened. I asked, 'Bunny, how are you?' She wept for about an hour. She just kept sobbing and saying over and over, 'Daddy, I didn't do anything wrong. I'm not a bad person.'" She cried and poured out her heart; it was her way of processing.

If he didn't have that heart name, "Bunny," the shell may have still been there. Probably she would have been going to games, cheerleading, and acting normal, but she would not have felt resolved.

Fourth Grade

Using a heart name when you are talking to a child about the trauma creates a safe and comforting place to discuss it. A lot of people will say, "I didn't have a pet name for my son. I didn't call him 'bookie smack' or something like that."

Did you have various sounds in your voice, when you were irritated and angry or warm and loving — a way you said his name when you were trying to be particularly tender with him? Even parents who don't use heart names will use different tones in different situations. Most children really have about five names based on the tone the parent uses at the time it is spoken. So use your tender voice, use your heart name voice when you ask a child about her or his trauma.

QUESTION 4.

When does my guiding some of my child's fourth-grade experiences turn into manipulation?

I feel like I just received a gem — the fourth-grade insights. I feel I might have received a weapon, too. Where does my focusing on this behavior turn into manipulation?

This is where unconditional love fits in and motive makes the difference. According to the Bible, on Judgment Day we won't only be judged on what we

Fourth Grade

did or didn't do, we'll also be judged on why we did or didn't do it. From my perspective, if my motive is to get my agenda accomplished, that's not good. But if my motive is to help my child do better in life, then that's not manipulation. Or at least it's justifiable manipulation (smile).

> **QUESTION 5.**
>
> *I've got a pre-K 4-year-old. I'm wondering how much of this I can use with him?*

BOBB: The focus I would have with a pre-K child is unconditional love. We would really focus on unconditional love and keep telling him you love him over and over — no matter what he does. You really love him. You enjoy being with him.

Then do things that promote bonding. When I was raising little ones that age, I had no clue. I was 21 years old when our first child was born. I wasn't smart enough to be married, much less to have a child or know what to do with that child. Today, when I see many parents reading to their daughters and sons and I see the bond that is forming, I think this is wonderful. It's incredible!

I had a client who adopted a set of twins. I talked to him about the concept of bonding with his children. I told him what I didn't do but wished I had. I didn't know quite what to do with them. I told him that if

Fourth Grade

he would spend an hour a day with them, he would be happy he did in the long term. His kids are now more than a decade older, and he's said that's the best advice anyone has ever given him. Because he spends an hour a day with his kids, he has grown to really love them. They look forward to that time. He looks forward to that time. Their hearts have really bonded together.

Life confidence in a person develops — or does not develop — before children ever go to school. If children feel their parents love them without condition, they go to school with life confidence. They know that their parents will still love them even if they do not perform perfectly. Life is OK. If you give children that kind of attention and love, it gives them a life confidence deep inside. Then when they go to school, they're prepared. It doesn't matter what school life throws at them. They know they have the security of your love and care.

However, those children who sense no love, or conditional love ("I'll love you if ...") or inconsistent love ("I love you when I'm sober and beat you when I'm drunk"), at home have to wear a mask of false confidence when they go to school. Life is not OK, but they put on a show so others do not see they are uncertain and afraid. They develop situational confidence; they are confident in certain situations but feel generally insecure in the rest of life. A child who receives inconsistent or conditional love may feel that he or she has to perform to get love or may feel he or she cannot depend on being loved.

Tell children you love them. Children are not good guessers. But they assume (often incorrectly) a lot! Do not make children guess whether you love them or not. We are not just talking about your own children, but your grandchildren, your nieces or nephews, even kids in your Sunday School class, your Scout troop, or wherever you're working with children.

> **QUESTION 6.**
>
> *My family moved out of state and I didn't carry any of the relationships with friends or teachers from fourth grade to the fifth grade. Does that create any special issues?*

It really does. Sometimes people experience a split in the fourth grade. For example, you may have been a leader in the first half of the fourth grade. The teachers liked you. The other students followed you. You were even a leader in the classroom. Then your parent's work situation changed, and your family moved. In the new school no one knew you, and you were totally alone in the last half of the fourth grade. You got picked on at the playground, felt behind in the classroom, etc.

When a child moves halfway through the fourth grade, often they develop two very different levels of confidence, which often, as an adult, confuses them and their spouse. In some social settings they feel very

Fourth Grade

confident and strong. In other social settings they seem insecure, shy, reclusive.

BOBB: I am often asked, "Why do I as president of our firm feel so insecure in certain social settings?" I ask, "Did you change schools in the fourth grade?" You guessed the answer: "Yes!" Then I explain that any time this adult gets into a social setting that reminds her or him of the first school, they feel very relaxed and confident. But when they are in a social setting that reminds them of the second school, they feel insecure and want to avoid the setting. This is a pattern we've seen dozens of times. It is very predictable.

A 38-year-old missionary's wife said, "When I was in the first half of my fourth grade, I was the leader. I was confident. I was happy. I was excited about life. Everything was grand, but then when I got to the last half of the fourth grade, my girlfriends started making fun of me because I couldn't go to movies. I was raised a conservative Christian. They started making fun of me and I just went into a shell and I've been there ever since. What does that mean?"

I said, "What it means is the real you is a confident person. Much more confident than you appear to be. Much more confident than you feel today. Do you have a picture of yourself from when you were in the fourth grade? Take that picture of you from when you were confident, when you felt really good about yourself and good about life and you had lots of friends. Put that picture somewhere in your home as an everyday reminder of what you have the capacity to be: the real you."

Six months later we met again and I could hardly recognize her as the same person. You could feel her confidence. She said, "You'll never know what it meant just having the picture there. Remembering brings back that comfort zone of what I was in the fourth grade."

If you had a split experience in fourth grade, I suggest you try to remember what it was like to be with your friends. Do you have any pictures of you with them or of that house or before you moved? Show your spouse the pictures and tell him or her what it felt like when you were in the fourth grade here and what it felt like there. Help your spouse understand the difference within, because half of you may be really confident and half of you feels socially very insecure regardless of your current position or income level.

> **QUESTION 7.**
>
> *What have you observed as to how we as parents might capitalize on this window in a spiritual sense with our children?*
>
> *Obviously, we're all concerned about them coming to know Jesus Christ as their Lord and Savior, and developing a deep personal relationship with the Lord and it sounds like this is a very good time either to capitalize upon that or to become deeply rooted as a Christian. Even as a small child that will carry them through their life.*

Fourth Grade

BOBB: It's a great question. I have spent many days one-on-one with many of the great Christian leaders of our generation. I've asked many of them how old they were when they accepted Christ. One of the very common ages is 9.

First, second, and third grades are great for spiritual learning, too. It doesn't mean they can't accept Christ before age 9. Younger children may understand spiritual realities to the level their "little hearts will let them," as my mother would say. But by the time they're 8 or 9, they get it on a whole different level, instead of at a naive elementary level. You're still the hero with your children at age 9, unlike maybe at 19. I'm not predicting teenage trauma here, but I am saying that at age 9 they still listen to you carefully and still believe what you tell them. That's the time to talk to them. Many of today's spiritual leaders made deep spiritual commitments that early and they feel it wasn't just a childhood gesture. They feel like their conversion at age 8 or 9 was a very genuine experience.

QUESTION 8.

What will be the result if my fourth-grade boy is surrounded by women?

What if he is raised by his mother, has a woman teacher, has a woman Sunday school teacher, and seems to be surrounded by females?

Fourth Grade

BOBB: It would be ideal if this boy could have a caring male role model somewhere in his life at age 9.

I am on the road a lot, so I'm not at our home church often enough to teach Sunday School consistently.

If I were to teach, most people would assume I'd teach young couples or young adults leaders. But I wouldn't teach any of them. I would only want to teach fourth-graders. I want to work with fourth-graders because I think they need adult male images at that age.

When I was a kid, we didn't have any male teachers in elementary school. Not one. Now they have male elementary teachers even in the small towns. We did have Boy Scouts; we had Christian Scout leaders who were men that worked with us, went camping with us. So even if I hadn't had a dad working with me, I would have had male role models.

The implication, though, is that the child will grow up very sensitive to women or very resentful of them. If the women in his life are caring and trustworthy, the child will be very comfortable with women. He will trust women, but if the women have an underlying distrust of men, that boy will grow up with a distrust of men. If the women are cold or uncaring, that child will grow up resentful of women.

Fourth Grade

> **QUESTION 9.**
>
> *What can parents do so each child gets an opportunity to lead and to follow?*
>
> *I'd like to ask about your discussion about whether we were the leaders in our home or we were never able to lead as a fourth-grader. I have a unique situation: I have a set of triplets. It's kind of a social experiment in that my set of triplets has been raised in the same environment, yet it's been interesting to see the hierarchy that has already been established and they're only 4. What can parents do to sort of engineer their minds so that each of them gets an opportunity to lead as opposed to one always being the follower?*

BOBB: I wrote a book called *Why You Do What You Do*. In the book, I make the point that no two children are ever raised in the same home, emotionally.

- Every child has a unique relationship with her or his father and mother.
- Each has unique relationships with other siblings.
- Each reminds family members more of "Dad's side of the family" or "Mom's side of the family."
- Each has a different personality that affects their world differently and gets different feedback from their fourth-grade world:

"You are a good kid ... a troublemaker ... smart ... slow," etc.
- Each becomes comfortable in different zones!

There's always someone that says, "Wow, is that good news, because all my life insensitive people have sarcastically asked, 'You were raised in the same home as your brother. How did you turn out so different?'" Thereby implying he was such a winner and you are such a loser!

The reality is that no children are raised in the same home emotionally. Not even triplets.

Remember, there are three reasons why we are the way we are: heredity, environment, and personal decisions. One of your triplets may have more of your genes or your spouse's genes, or may just be a more dominant person who wants to take over. Perhaps a couple of them may be problem solvers. They say, "You set the goals and we'll solve the problem."

Triplets may have a natural compatibility, but even with triplets I would occasionally separate them in the fourth grade. Let them play separately. They may not want to be separated. I would not separate them for the whole fourth grade, but at least for an evening here and an evening there, or I'd let one of them sleep at one friend's house and the other one sleep at another friend's house without taking all three. Let each of the three get an individual sense of leading, following, and relating without always being part of a threesome.

Fourth Grade

Make sure to give each of the triplets a different heart name. When you're alone, one-on-one, call them by their heart name, so each one feels that "each of my parents knows me and I have a very unique and special relationship with them."

> **QUESTION 10.**
>
> *I'm home schooling. What if my fourth-grader can't seem to concentrate?*

BOBB: A client of mine memorized massive amounts of material. I asked him, "What's the key to memory?" He said, "Concentration! If you can't concentrate, you can't memorize."

The first thing I would do with this child is take a break and just ask, "What's on your mind?" Just let her or him talk for a while and get some of the painful thoughts and feelings out where you can talk about them.

Sometimes in a session with a client, we'll get to a point where he or she can't even focus because they are very distracted by something on the desk or outside the window, or someone walking past. There are too many things running through the client's brain. Often, we encourage a five-minute break. Then we ask her or him to get paper and a pencil and write down everything that is on their mind at the moment.

Fourth Grade

Everything he or she
>should have done,
>meant to do,
>didn't do,
>ought to do…

an exhaustive list of everything that is heavy on her/his shoulders.

On average, clients will make a list of 75 things in five minutes. "I should have written my mother, I should have called my dad, I should have checked with the bank on this, I should have done that, I should have bought this." When a client gets them all out, we say, "Now, they're down. You're not going to forget them. We can talk now."

Let your fourth-grader tell you all that is on her or his mind. Make a list and say, "We can do those when we're done here."

The other thing is, you may want to examine the distractions in the environment — toys, video games, moving objects, etc. Would there be other rooms in the house or other places on your property where the child would be able to concentrate better?

When I consult with a company president, if we work in the office it is very difficult for the person to concentrate. The phone rings, someone knocks needing immediate input or decisions made, etc. If we have time, I'll say, "Hey, we've got some time, can we go for a ride?" Often when a president is driving down the road, he or she will sit there and

Fourth Grade

talk a steady stream. He or she is clear. There's little defensiveness. You get what's in the person's heart. When you get back to the office, those interruptions and nagging reminders begin to creep back into the conversation.

Be aware of the possibility that you've stumbled onto a learning problem. If it's a consistent pattern where you give the person a verbal cue and he or she can't respond to you, there may be a deeper issue. Discuss testing options with the local school counselor or a learning specialist.

Remember when we said you want to be a cheerleader rather than a critic? Particularly if your fourth-grader is smart, which most of them are. Tell them how smart they are.

A client, a president of a bank, told me he wasn't smart. I had a hard time convincing him otherwise. I told him that I've consulted with hundreds of presidents and thousands of executive staff people, and that he was a very smart, accomplished man. I asked, "Why do you think you're slow?" His confession? "Because Mom said I was. 'You're not smart like your brother. You're just slow.'" I assured him, "You're anything but slow. You're a very smart man."

Incidentally, one of the distinctions many who wrestle with feeling "dumb" have found helpful is the distinction between smart and academic. Many top leaders are very smart but for some reason didn't, and still wouldn't, do well in the classroom. They end up doing very well in life but never have adjusted to the classroom setting.

And many in the classroom have very strong disciplines and get great grades, making them appear to be far smarter than an IQ test would actually show them to be.

Everyone is smart. Here's how you can know where you are smart. Answer this question:

> ***What do you find very easy or obvious that others don't seem to get quickly — or at all?***

This is the area in which you are smart.

With your fourth-graders, be sure to tell her or him, "You are smart!" If you tell kids they're smart, they'll believe you. If you do not, they may conclude incorrectly that they are "dumb" because some jealous bully said so.

Remember: to a child, perception is reality!

SAY "THANK YOU!"

When you were in the fourth grade, someone shaped your life or you would not be where you are today! Who shaped your life the most? Consider writing that person a note or paying him or her a personal visit. Say "Thank you!" while they are still living.

Fourth Grade

BOBB: The teacher, Aulene Neeland, who shaped my life the very most, died before I was old enough to realize I should say "thank you." If your most influential person has died, it is not too late to go to the place where he or she is buried. You are not talking to a spirit. You are talking to your memory of her or him. You can just say, "I am coming here in respect to say 'thank you' for shaping my life, for caring about me, for loving me, for teaching me."

You could also write down what you learned from this person who shaped your life in the fourth grade. Perhaps you might get an artist to help you make it look pretty. Give it to the person you want to thank, or give it to his or her children or grandchildren if the person has died. You can say, for example, "Your grandfather was like a grandfather to me, and here's what he taught me. I would like to make it available to you."

Say "thank you" because
age 9
(typically, the fourth grade)
was
the tipping point
of your adult comfort zones
as a human being.

Fourth Grade

A SIGNIFICANT DIFFERENCE
See the insights in this book as ones that apply not only to your children but also to the children with your children, the children in your Sunday school, the children on your street, your nieces and nephews. Start building security into them. Love them and be their cheerleader.

It will make a very significant difference!

ONE FINAL QUESTION:

> If you were 100 percent convinced
> that the fourth grade is the
> single most shaping year
> of a human being's existence (like we are),
> what would you actually
> do differently?

PLEASE ... DO IT!

Bobb and Emőke

F. WRAP-UP

REMEMBER as you think of your own fourth-grader(s):

Your unconditional love gives your child confidence to learn and grow in any area of life.

Your child (male or female) will benefit decades into the future by:

1. Learning to play an instrument (ideally an instrument they would enjoy as adults).

2. Learning social manners (at the meal table, in polite society, at formal events, etc.).

3. Learning to enjoy learning (at school and/or elsewhere).

4. Learning to play with older kids (learning to follow) and younger kids (learning to lead).

5. Learning to enjoy social life outside of school (in church, clubs or teams).

6. Learning to be comfortable financially (with kids who have more money and less money).

7. Learning to relate to each brother and sister (in a healthy way — may need help here).

8. Learning to play with boys and girls (being

Fourth Grade

comfortable with men and women as adults).

9. Learning to process loss in competition (looking for what to do differently or better next time).

10. Learning to make money beyond allowance (learning the value of a hard-earned dollar).

Obviously, not all of these are required to be successful adults. But these learning experiences in the fourth grade will help your child be far more comfortable in these areas as adults.

We would like to wish you Godspeed with your fourth-graders!

Bobb and Emőke

Fourth Grade

Fourth Grade

An introduction ... and an invitation!

As an executive mentor/consultant, I have the rare privilege of spending days at a time with some of the finest leaders of our generation. I continue to grow personally, learning more in the past year than I've learned in the five years before it.

Mentoring Realities

As you now know, I define mentoring as, ideally, "a lifelong relationship in which the mentor helps the protégé grow into their God-given potential over a lifetime." Realistically, because of schedule pressures, my personal mentoring is limited to a very few individuals. At the same time, I truly want to see friends like you grow into your God-given potential over your lifetime.

Solomon advised, "Get wisdom."

The search of today seems to be focused on becoming a courageous, charming, powerful, successful person. However, according to the Bible, Solomon, who was one of the wisest, if not the wisest, man that ever lived, gave us this profound and timeless bit of advice in Proverbs 4:5: GET WISDOM!

This is advice that our modern world seems to overlook. Enter the idea of **Quick Wisdom**. The focus of **Quick Wisdom** is to help you and your friends be WISE!

Today, it seems that every young leader I meet wants wisdom, but needs it fast. We don't have the time with today's pace and pressures to go to a mountaintop and study ancient manuscripts in Sanskrit. Thus my idea for quick access to timeless wisdom. My focus: weekly, I will send **Quick Wisdom** emails for you to read and pass on with the very best "wisdom nuggets" I can give you to help strengthen your protégés and friends.

Quick Wisdom is 100 percent free to you and your friends.

Fortunately, the email technology of today is such that you can enroll 10 friends or 100 to receive the Quick Wisdom email. It takes me the same amount of time to send you an email as it does to send it to all of your protégés and/or friends. I want to use my unique exposure to great wisdom to strengthen you and your friends for a lifetime.

Thank you, my friend, for telling your friends about **Quick Wisdom!**

To receive these FREE **Quick Wisdom** emails, simply visit BobbBiehl.com and sign up.

Fourth Grade

Helping you ...

... your children, your protégés and your staff — no matter what you do, no matter where you go, for the rest of your life — is the reason the following tools exist.

These tools are presented in five categories, each with five top tools:
- A. PERSONAL DEVELOPMENT
- B. LEADERSHIP DEVELOPMENT
- C. ORGANIZATIONAL DEVELOPMENT
- D. PLANNING
- E. GIFTS

A. PERSONAL DEVELOPMENT

1. NORTH STAR (video)
   Focusing your life — and keeping it focused.

   Focusing your next 50 years at the 50,000-foot level, in less than 50 minutes. Once focused, it is easy to refocus your life in a matter of minutes.

2. BUCKET LIST (video)
   Focusing your future — and keeping it in focus.

   What are the few measurable things you really want to get done — before you die? This is your *Bucket List!* This one video helps you create your personal bucket list in a very short period of time.

Fourth Grade

3. 4TH-GRADE(R) (book or video)
   Life's turning point.

   Fourth grade, age 9, is the single most shaping year of a person's existence. This DVD explains how your fourth grade shaped your life, or that of the staff member you are about to hire.

4. WHY YOU DO WHAT YOU DO (book)
   Understanding yourself and others.

   This book is a result of more than 50,000 hours of behind-the-smiles experiences with some of the finest leaders of our generation. It can help you better understand your spouse, your family members, and your team members.

5. DECADE BY DECADE (book)
   Life is surprisingly predictable.

   This book gives you a decade-by-decade understanding of what is "normal" for each decade of life, based on observing over 5,000 people personally over the last 45-plus years. This understanding helps bring perspective to what you are dealing with today.

B. LEADERSHIP DEVELOPMENT

6. ASKING PROFOUND QUESTIONS (booklet)
   Getting to the heart of an issue — fast!

   This confidence-building booklet contains more than 100 profound questions to help you deal

Fourth Grade

effectively with life 24 hours a day, seven days a week, for the rest of your life.

7. ANNUAL BALANCE CALENDAR (video)
   Balancing your life, personal and professional.

   This one simple DVD helps you find and keep far more balance between your personal and your professional life! Once your life is in balance, you have a clear context for daily, weekly, monthly, and quarterly effectiveness.

8. LEADING WITH CONFIDENCE (book)
   For the rest of your life.

   A wise, proven investment in your own future, covering 30 essential leadership areas, including:

   HOW TO COPE WITH change, depression, failure, fatigue, and pressure.

   HOW TO BECOME MORE attractive, balanced, confident, creative, disciplined, and motivated.

   HOW TO DEVELOP SKILLS IN asking, dreaming, goal setting, prioritizing, risk taking, influencing, money managing, personal organization, problem solving, decision making, and communicating.

   HOW TO BECOME MORE EFFECTIVE IN delegating, firing, reporting, team building, people building, recruiting, strategic planning, and motivating.

Fourth Grade

9. LEADERSHIP ACADEMY (24-DVD series)
Proven at all levels.

This series (24 DVDs and an accompanying series of handouts in a notebook) is the essence of the leadership tools, processes, and principles every leader needs, at all levels of leadership. These tools are scalable from the smallest startup group up to the president of any nation. This material comes from 45-plus years and thousands of hours of consulting with over 500 organizations. These DVDs will help strengthen you as a leader — for the rest of your life!

10. MENTORING (book)
How to find a mentor and how to become one.

If you would like to find a mentor or become a mentor but don't know where to start, this is the place! This book explains clearly what mentoring is, what mentors do and don't do, the nature of the mentor-protégé relationship, the most common roadblocks to effective mentoring, and much more.

ORGANIZATIONAL DEVELOPMENT

11. BOARDROOM CONFIDENCE (book)
First board or 10th board.

If you are considering serving on a board, are already on a board, or are the chairperson leading a board, *Boardroom Confidence* is a valuable and proven tool to help you and your board serve with confidence!

12. OPPORTUNITY-SPOTTING QUESTIONS (video)
Opportunity – key to explosive growth!

Opportunity-Spotting Questions is a shockingly simple series of profound questions that can help you spot high-potential opportunities everyone on your team — including you — is overlooking.

13. STOP SETTING GOALS (book)
If you prefer solving problems!

Within 100 miles of you at this moment: approximately 15 percent of adults are naturally energized by GOALS! Approximately 80 percent are naturally energized by PROBLEMS! Approximately five percent are naturally energized by OPPORTUNITIES!

This insight is a critical understanding for anyone in any leadership or management position who is responsible for motivating and maximizing a team.

14. TEAM PROFILE (self-scoring inventory)
Getting "round pegs in round holes."

The *Team Profile* lets you tell others:
    What makes you tick!
    What turns you on!
    What burns you out!

Fourth Grade

It helps each team member define her or his ideal role on the team and is key to building a successful team. It helps you get "round pegs in round holes."

15. FIRING STAR (video)
Firing a team member — in a "Christian way."

Firing Star helps you release a staff person in a humane way. The way in which they are released makes a huge difference. *Firing Star* helps you know how to release a person in the way you would want to be released!

PLANNING

16. STRATEGIC PLANNING ARROW
(24" x 36" sheet)
Your team's future direction, on one sheet of paper.

The *Strategic Planning Arrow* is a proven tool for helping teams define a clear team direction. When a team is making the same basic assumptions about direction, it dramatically reduces the frustration, pressure, and tension the team is experiencing on a day-to-day basis! (Formerly titled: "Masterplanning Arrow.")

17. STRATEGIC PLANNING (book)
Step-by-step planning process.

By reading one book, your whole team can have one proven, step-by-step planning process they all understand, regardless of background. Proven in hundreds of organizations, divisions, and departments with a wide variety of leadership styles. (Formerly titled: "Masterplanning.")

18. SPEED PLANNING (video)
When you have one to three planning hours, not one to three days.

Whenever you are running short on time but still need to focus your team, this is a very helpful tool. It doesn't help you put together a 30-page plan, but it quickly gives your team focus on a couple of sheets.

19. VITAL SIGNS AND CRITICAL STANDARDS (video)
Keeping your organization healthy.

The *Vital Signs and Critical Standards* video helps you quickly tell if your organization is healthy, if you should be concerned, or if your organization is in real trouble! At your option, you can also give these charts to your board, reassuring them or alerting them to major problems.

20. PROCESS CHARTING (video)
Key to transferability.

When any responsibility, program, or organization is transferred from one person to the next, process is the secret of effectively transferring the responsibility.

Fourth Grade

GIFTS

21. ON MY OWN (book)
    Perfect gift for graduation.

    If you have been increasingly concerned about your high school or college student's readiness to face the "real world," this book has been written for the students in your world. These principles will stay with them for a lifetime, and they can pass them on to their children's children.

22. LEADERSHIP INSIGHTS (book)
    Perfect gift for young executives.

    Leadership Insights contains the 101 insights, principles, definitions, and rules of thumb that can help you in any type of work — for the rest of your life!

23. DATING QUESTIONS (book)
    Perfect gift for couples beginning to date seriously.

    This gift book teaches any young couple 250 fun questions to ask BEFORE they get engaged or married. It will help both of them know the real person "behind the smile" — before asking "Will you?" or answering "I will!" (Formerly titled: "Should We Get Married?")

24. HEAVEN (book)
    Perfect gift for hospice care or grieving.

    Heaven gives deep comfort to any person facing

imminent death or grieving the loss of a loved one. Reading *Heaven* helps a person imagine what heaven could be like in a vivid, inviting, and comforting way.

25. MEMORIES (album-/heirloom-type books)
Perfect gift for parents or grandparents.

The *Memories* book contains 500-plus memory-jogging questions to help your loved one remember and write about her or his life experiences. It's a beautiful album-type book with padded covers and a binding that opens widely for easy writing. It's a great birthday or Christmas gift for any living parent, grandparent, aunt, uncle, or mentor!

Helping you continue
growing into your full potential
and
building your family or team
is the reason each of these tools exist.

They are all available at BobbBiehl.com.

Here to help turn your dreams into reality,

Bobb

Bobb Biehl
Coach, Consultant, Executive Mentor

Fourth Grade

Coach — Teaching specific skills.
Consultant — Helping leaders build organizations.
Executive Mentor — A lifelong relationship, helping an executive you believe in reach their God-given potential.

©2022 Bobb Biehl — www.BobbBiehl.com